YOSHI
AND
ME

How a Golden Dog Taught Me to Stay

YEVETTE HO

 www.yopaws.com.au

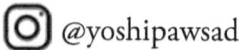 @yoshipawsad

 YoshiPawsAD

© 2025 Yevette Ho

All rights reserved. No part of this publication may be reproduced, stored in a retrieval system, or transmitted in any form or by any means, electronic, mechanical, photocopying, recording, or otherwise, without prior written permission of the author, except for brief quotations used in reviews or critical articles.

First published in 2025 by Vetz Media Publishing

Canberra, Australia

Table of Contents

Preface: Not a Guidebook: A Survival Map	v
How to Read This Book	vi
Our Story: Our Why	vi
A Note to You	vii
Part 1	**1**
1. Breathing Through the Wreckage	3
2. The Moment There Was No Help	6
3. The Golden Retriever in an Apartment	10
4. Why Relationship Comes First: Before the Cue	19
5. The Hard Days	24
6. The Day Everything Broke	27
i. Not Just Property but My Everything	27
ii. Aftermath	31
7. Finding Our Team	37
8. Tasks She Taught Herself: Because She's Magic	45
9. Rewriting My Days: Around Her Paws	51
10. Paperwork, Perfection: and Puppyhood	56
11. People Are the Problem	62
12. Yoshi Wasn't the Problem	70
13. The Shape of Resilience	75
14. Yoshi's Social Life Is Better Than Mine	81
15. Juggling, Joy and Just Showing Up	88
16. When People Hurt, She Heals	96

Part 2	103
17. Breeder vs Rescue: I Just Wanted the Right Dog	105
18. Owner-Trained vs Organisation-Trained: Choosing Our Own Path	111
19. What They Don't Tell You: About Owner-Training	114
20. Plateau Brain, Puppy Heart: When Training Feels Stuck	121
21. So You Want to Train Your Own Assistance Dog: Getting Started the Smart Way	124
22. Practising for the Public: The First Outing Is Never the First	133
23. Not Quite Ready: But Getting Closer	139
24. Why We're Not Rushing the Test	142
25. Training Through the Spiral	147
26. Where to Next: Building Toward Certification (If That's Your Goal)	150
27. Intro to Advanced Training: Tasks & Troubleshooting	156
28. Becoming, Together	164

Epilogue: Still here, Still us

PREFACE

Not a Guidebook: A Survival Map

This book might feel a little all over the place because honestly, so is life with invisible illness and an assistance dog.

When I needed something like this, it didn't exist. So I didn't write a step-by-step manual I wrote the book I wish I'd had. I wanted people to know the truth: the messy, exhausting, beautiful truth of living with a disability, training your own dog, and carrying on even when the world insists you're not 'sick enough,' 'disabled enough,' or 'doing it the right way.'

There's so much information out there, and somehow… still not enough. So many options that aren't really options. So many doors that only open if you say the magic words.

I could've stuck to the facts and skipped the feelings. But that wouldn't have shown what it feels like to cry into your dog's fur at 3am, or to face yet another closed door with nothing but stubborn hope and a leash in your hand.

So this is part story, part survival map. Not a pity party but a mirror and a megaphone.

To say:

- Yes, it's hard.
- Yes, bad things happen to people like us.
- No, you're not weak for needing help.

If Yoshi and I with scraped knees and an overstuffed poop bag can keep going, maybe you can too. Maybe with a little help. Maybe with four paws beside you.

We're still learning. Still growing. Still breathing together. And if we can do that, so can you.

How to Read This Book

There are no rules. Start in the middle. Skip around. Come back later.

This isn't a guidebook. It's lived experience: jagged, soft, funny, frustrating, unfinished. Just like life. Especially life with chronic illness, trauma, and a slightly-too-honest dog.

Read it sideways. Read it out loud to your dog. Cry if you need to. Laugh when you can. You don't need fixing; you just need reminding:

You're still here. And maybe that's enough for today.

Our Story: Our Why

Writing this was scary. But I couldn't stop thinking about the person wide awake at 2am, scrolling through the noise, just hoping to find something. I know that feeling. I've been there. That's why I wrote this.

Living with invisible illness means navigating a world that wasn't built for you. It is a world filled with paperwork, fatigue, and misunderstanding. Adding an assistance dog into the mix? Chaos, paperwork, and magic.

Yoshi isn't just 'a dog.' She's my teammate. My lifeline. She doesn't ask for explanations. She just shows up. Over and over again.

This isn't a neat story. It's detours, heartbreak, small wins, and unexpected lessons. But if we can do this, maybe you can too.

A Note to You

For anyone just trying to stay upright, juggling paperwork, poop bags, panic, and a puppy who thinks socks are currency…

If you've whispered, 'I can't do this', but did it anyway; This is for you.

Yoshi and I are just one scrappy team among many. But if our story makes you feel seen, that's a win.

You're not alone. (And if you are… we hope you brought snacks.)

With love,

Yevette & Yoshi

CHAPTER 1

Breathing Through the Wreckage

The first time Yoshi told me I couldn't breathe, I didn't believe her. She padded over, rested her chin and paw on my arm, and stared like she was waiting for me to notice something. Five minutes later, my lungs collapsed into a wheezing fit so violent my pulse oximeter flashed oxygen levels in the 80s and a heart rate climbing past 150.

That's the thing about life with an assistance dog, sometimes they see the wreckage before you even realise you're standing in it.

It starts with exhaustion. Not the 'I stayed up too late watching Netflix' kind. The soul-deep, bone-heavy weariness that makes brushing your teeth feel like a marathon. Every joint aches. Muscles twitch. Skin burns. Everything hurts and you start wondering if maybe you're not even really alive. Just a shell. Moving, breathing, surviving but no longer living.

That's where I was.

Doctors couldn't agree on what was wrong. PTSD. Anxiety. Maybe chronic pain. Maybe autoimmune. Maybe 'just stress.' One told me to get a hobby. Another suggested essential oils. And in that moment, all I wanted to do was scream.

What I needed was help. Real help. The kind you cannot bottle or DIY. But invisible disabilities confuse people. If you do not 'look sick,' you must be okay. Right? Wrong. I was unravelling. And no one saw it.

In desperation, I started researching assistance dogs. Not because I wanted a pet because I needed a partner. Someone who could help me navigate panic attacks, sensory overload, dissociation. Someone steady. Reliable. Non-judgmental.

For more than 20 years, I had told people, "I can't even take care of myself, how could I care for a dog?"

But now it felt like my only shot.

It wasn't about adding more responsibility. It was about survival.

I was slipping through the cracks again. Maybe four paws could hold me together where people couldn't.

I even caught myself wondering: Would the dog live longer than I would?

I never wanted a dog before 55 because I didn't think I'd make it past 65. But right then, I didn't even think I'd make it through the year.

Finding help in a system built for visibility was just the beginning of a harder lesson.

 **Pawnote**

Could a Dog Help? If you're wondering whether an assistance dog could help, ask yourself:

- Are you struggling with tasks related to your disability?
- Would a dog-trained task reduce your need for paid supports?
- Do you need help with emotional regulation, mobility, alerts, or safety?

You don't have to wait for permission to need help. Sometimes help looks like four paws and a waggy tail.

Extra Tips:

- Look at what your hardest days are like. Could a dog make those just 5 percent more bearable?
- Assistance dogs don't have to be perfect. Neither do you.
- You're not 'failing' if you need help. That's what this dog is for.

 WARNING: If you're considering an assistance dog because you're overwhelmed, make sure to line up support for the *dog's* needs too. Puppies do not magically fix things, but the right partnership can create a foundation to build from.

CHAPTER 2

The Moment There Was No Help

(NDIS: Not Designed for Invisible Struggles)

Ah yes. The NDIS. Or Centrelink. Or any service that says it helps people like me.

Unless, of course, your disability isn't photogenic enough.

I did everything they asked. I called. I explained. I applied. I cried. I documented every meltdown, shutdown, symptom, and fear.

GP letters. Specialist reports. Psych assessments. Letters from professionals who knew me and my reality.

And still, 'You're managing.'
'Not quite eligible.'
'Have you tried joining a group?'

Join a group? People are the reason I don't leave the house. Noise, unpredictability, crowds — they are not just inconvenient. They are dangerous. Triggering.

So no, I am not managing. Unless managing means: Sobbing in the shower, Living off toast because cooking is too hard.

Freezing in the pharmacy because someone brushed past me and my system collapsed.

Then sure. Let's pretend I'm thriving.

But surviving is not the same as living.

When I asked about support for assistance dog training, the rejections got colder.

'Are you a veteran?'
'A first responder?'
'Did you serve?'

No, I didn't wear their uniform. But I worked with those who did. I fought alongside them. Protected their teams. But that didn't matter.

I was just a security contractor. Just a civilian with PTSD, agoraphobia, autism, and pain. Not broken the right way.

Try a support group, they said. Even those were reserved for veterans only.

Every door slammed shut. Every rejection was another reminder: You don't count.

So I stopped asking.

And I started alone.

No funding. No help. No guidance.

Just me.

And soon, a lifeline came wrapped in fur, hope, and a little bit of Chaos. Her name was Yoshi.

> 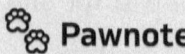 **Pawnote**
>
> **DDA vs NDIS**
>
> 📄 **DDA (Disability Discrimination Act):**
> - Covers access rights.
> - Allows you to take a trained assistance dog into public places (if the dog is under control, trained to assist your disability, and hygienic).
>
> 🐾 **NDIS (National Disability Insurance Scheme):**
>
> Funding is only provided if:
> - You have a formally assessed need.
> - The dog is trained by or through a recognised provider.
> - You meet all requirements around documentation, goals, standards, and review processes.
>
> The irony is that while NDIS often rejects funding for assistance dogs, investing in treatment and support early, including properly trained dogs, actually saves money in the long run. It reduces hospital visits, crisis interventions, and other high-cost supports.
>
> 🚫 **Translation:**
> - Your dog can be legal without being NDIS-funded.
> - NDIS approval is not guaranteed, even if the dog satisfies all DDA standards

What can you do?

- Document everything.
- Keep a journal of the dog's training, tasks, behaviour, and your symptoms.
- Use that data to support your case.

EXTRA TIP: Even without NDIS funding, you can still train your own dog. Many trainers and programs will support 'owner-trainers' with flexible options.

CHAPTER 3

The Golden Retriever in an Apartment

Choosing a dog isn't just about cuteness. It's about survival.

When you live with disability and getting out of bed feels like climbing Everest, you don't just need a companion. You need a partner… Someone who can help you hold it together when everything else falls apart. Someone who can ground you when you dissociate, steady you when panic spikes, and give you a reason to try again when you've got nothing left.

That's why I was so careful.

I knew what I needed: a small dog, ideally under 15kg. Low shedding, so my respiratory issues would not flare. Gentle temperament. Intelligent, trainable. A breed suited for assistance work and apartment living.

I searched for months. I asked questions. I read articles. I looked at reviews and testimonials. I messaged breeders, compared notes, made spreadsheets. Finally, I found one who promised exactly what I needed: a Toy Groodle 5-15kg, low-shedding, genetically clear.

The breeder sent photos. She sounded experienced. She reassured me that the pup would be suitable for my disability needs. That I wouldn't have to worry. That everything would be fine.

I believed her.

I paid the deposit.

I thought I'd done everything right.

And then Yoshi arrived.

She was tiny, sure. But something felt… off.

She was sick. Dull coat, dandruffy skin. Under-socialised. Her belly was bloated. She didn't play. She didn't explore. She just curled up and whimpered.

Then, the worms came. Crawling out of her. For two days straight.

The breeder brushed it off. 'That is normal,' she said, 'It probably came from the mother'. But why was the mother infested in the first place?

I started hearing from other people who had bought her siblings.

Some were noticing their puppies getting much bigger than expected. They messaged in group chats and forums, wondering aloud,

'Is my dog underweight?'
'Should she still be eating puppy food, or transitioning?'
'How do we know how much to feed if we don't know how big they're meant to get?'

And the truth was: we didn't know.
We couldn't know.

Because we weren't told the truth.

So I ordered a full DNA test.

And that's when the truth hit: Yoshi wasn't a Toy Groodle at all.

She was 100 percent Golden Retriever.

No Poodle. No Toy. Just Golden.

On top of that, the results showed she carried two copies of a gene linked to ichthyosis—a lifelong genetic skin condition that causes flaking, itchiness, and irritation. The breeder never mentioned this. Never screened for it. Never disclosed the risk.

We were devastated.

This was a complete misrepresentation, not simply a case of a dog being 'a bit bigger than expected.' We didn't know who her parents were. We didn't know what health issues might show up down the track. We didn't know how big she'd get. One of her siblings was part Labrador. Another was also a full Golden. There wasn't a drop of Poodle in any of them.

We were scammed.

And the breeder? She disappeared.

When I contacted Fair Trading, they told me they couldn't do anything unless the breeder responded to their requests. And she didn't.

Their advice? 'Take it to NCAT.'

That meant the New South Wales Civil and Administrative Tribunal (NCAT).
More money I didn't have.
More paperwork.
More stress.
More fighting… for something I never should have had to fight for in the first place.

But the impact wasn't abstract. It was real. Tangible. Ongoing.

When we finally went to the reconciliation hearing, the breeder actually turned up. She denied responsibility completely. She claimed the Australian Business Number (ABN) on the paperwork was not hers, that it belonged to her daughter who had supposedly run away.

The problem was, we had never met this daughter. We had only ever dealt with the breeder herself, from the first messages to the delivery of the dog. Every payment, every arrangement, every word had been with her. Yet suddenly she was blaming this mystery daughter, insisting she was nothing more than the person who delivered the dog.

During the private phone call where we were meant to work things out, she even said she wanted the dog back so she could give her to a dying family member as an assistance dog. I was outraged. After everything I had been through, after all the pain she had caused, this was what she came up with? And if it wasn't her business in the first place, what right did she have to even ask for the dog back?

When we returned to the mediator, I tried to explain. But I was shut down again and again. As an autistic person, I was already struggling to find the right words, to string my thoughts together. Instead of being heard, I was dismissed. My voice, my reality, was pushed aside.

NCAT told us that unless the daughter was served with the orders, nothing could proceed. It didn't matter that the daughter's address was the same as her mother's. It didn't matter that the breeder sitting right in front of me was the one I had dealt with the whole time.

And so, as unbelievable as it sounds, this fraud will get away with it, protected by a lie and a loophole.

Yoshi now weighs over 26 kilograms, and that's underweight, according to the vet. She's a full-sized working breed in a one-bedroom apartment.

She sheds constantly. Thick, golden clouds. It gets in my throat, clogs the air purifier, aggravates my allergies. I'm on daily antihistamines now, and occasionally need to adjust my medication just to manage breathing, itching, and pain.

I live with chronic illness. With autoimmune issues, pain, fatigue, and trauma. I don't have family to help. I don't have a partner. It is just me.

The Golden Retriever in an Apartment

I needed a dog that would make life more manageable, not harder. But this? This was crushing.

I considered rehoming her. I did. Not once, not twice, maybe a few dozen times.

But by then, it was already too late.

She was mine. Bonded. Attached. The critical 8 to 12 week socialisation window had already passed. And more importantly, she was already helping me.

Despite her rough start, despite the trauma, despite the size and shedding and chaos, she became my assistance dog. The bond we built was intense. Deep. Lifesaving.

I didn't choose to keep her out of convenience. I kept her because we were a team.

Because she was already alerting to pain. Already grounding me. Already sensing my spirals before I could even name them.

But the costs kept stacking up. A big dog means big bills.

There was the bigger food budget, special allergy friendly meals, supplements, grooming, vet care, cleaning supplies, and endless lint rollers. On top of that came training sessions, memberships, and even hiring fields for exercise.

It might sound unusual to some to pay for a field, yet living in a very small apartment meant Yoshi had nowhere safe to run or practice her skills off leash. She needed a controlled, fenced space where she could zoom, learn, and burn off energy without risk. For a puppy in training, that space was not a luxury. It was essential.

Everything costs more.

And me? I'm working every hour I can. But it's not enough.

Some days, I cry because I'm too sick to work, but too broke to stop.

Some days I think I cannot do this anymore. Some nights, I wonder if I'll have to give her up—not because I want to, but because I physically, financially, emotionally can't keep up.

This wasn't what I signed up for.

I relied on the breeder's claims to make an informed decision. One that directly impacted my health, my finances, my safety. Instead, I've been left overwhelmed, unwell, and heartbroken.

I did everything right. But the system failed me. And now, I'm the one paying for someone else's lies.

Still somehow, we keep going.

Because in between the setbacks, the pain, the chaos… There's love.

Big, clumsy, golden love.

🐾 Pawnote

When the Dog You Get Isn't the Dog You Planned For

💔 First, Feel It:

It's okay to grieve the dog you thought you were getting. You're not ungrateful, you're human. Misrepresentation, accidents, or unexpected needs can hit hard. Acknowledge the disappointment before it turns into resentment.

🐕 It's Not Their Fault:

Your dog didn't choose their breed, size, or health issues. They're just being who they are. Try to separate frustration at the situation from how you see your dog.

📚 Learn the Dog You Have:

- Research their breed traits and health needs. Do not rely on generic advice.
- Adjust your expectations to match their reality, not the sales pitch you were given.
- Build a care plan that works for both your limitations and their energy levels.

💡 Shift the Focus:

Instead of 'What can't we do?' try 'What *can* we do together?' Sometimes the bond that grows from adapting is deeper than the one you imagined.

CHAPTER 4

Why Relationship Comes First: Before the Cue

Some days, training feels like a magical dance. You ask, they respond. You cue, they succeed. Everyone feels like a genius. But then there are the other days. The ones where nothing works. Where the leash tangles, your dog forgets her own name, and the neighbours get a free performance of your emotional collapse in activewear.

One time, I spent an hour practicing 'heel' outside a café. Yoshi did great… until a rogue napkin fluttered across the footpath and she absolutely lost it. Tail up, body stiff, the napkin was clearly a Level 5 Threat. She barked once. Then again. People stared. Someone laughed.

She wanted to bolt in the other direction and honestly, so did I. I panicked. Being out in public was already hard enough. Managing my own anxiety, pain, and overstimulation is a full-time job on its own. But now my dog, the one who was meant to help me, was struggling too. She wasn't calming me. She was spiralling. And in that moment, it felt like I had failed both of us.

But here's the thing: she comes first. No matter how overwhelmed I am, she's still a young dog learning to navigate a world that often doesn't make sense to her either. She wasn't being difficult. She was scared. She needed connection, not correction. And that's what I had to give.

She looked up at me like, *'We're okay, right?'* And in that moment, I realised something important: this is a long game. A forever kind of learning. Not a checklist.

We talk so much about training cues, schedules, and behaviours, but here's the truth, no one tells you loudly enough:

Before training comes trust. Before correction comes connection.

Rules without relationship creates rebellion.

If your dog doesn't feel safe with you, really safe, they won't follow you. Not because they're stubborn. Because the bond isn't there yet.

You can't build a solid house without laying a foundation. With dogs, that foundation is relationship. It starts with listening. Meeting their needs. Showing up consistently. Being their safe place in a chaotic world.

Training is not a six-week course. It's not something you finish. It's not a race to obedience. It's a lifelong conversation. A relationship that deepens over time.

When Yoshi looks to me now, I see that trust. I feel that connection. But we earned it together, slowly, awkwardly, honestly.

Training is already a mountain. Raising a puppy while chronically ill, neurodivergent, in pain, exhausted, and completely on your own? That's Everest, during a storm. Still, we tried. We failed. We tried again. And that was enough.

Why Relationship Comes First: Before the Cue

Yoshi and Me

Going to NCAT meant more money I did not have. More paperwork. More stress. More fighting for something I never should have had to fight for in the first place.

But the impact was not abstract. It was real. It still is.

I have given up on NCAT. The process that was meant to protect me only left me drained. They told me to hire a private investigator, as if that was a realistic option. With what money? I could barely keep up with the bills I already had. And even if I did find her, they said it would be hard to get anything from her if she had nothing.

She stole from me. She lied to me. She got away with it.

What matters right now is the dog in front of me. She doesn't need a perfect handler. She needs *me*. Present. Patient. Paying attention.

Why Relationship Comes First: Before the Cue

So we take it one moment at a time. One glance. One cuddle. One quiet walk in the dark. We're not just building skills. We're building us.

> 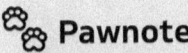 **Pawnote**
>
> **Training Isn't Linear** 🔄 **Reality check:**
>
> Progress isn't a straight line.
>
> Dogs have bad days (so do humans!)
>
> What they knew yesterday might be shaky today and that's normal.
>
> **⊠ What to do on 'off' days:**
>
> Go back to something easy and fun.
>
> Do a short session and end on a win.
>
> Skip formal training. Just play, cuddle or rest.

> **TRAINER TIP:** 'Repetition builds confidence. Success builds motivation. Struggle builds stress'. Choose success.
>
> 😊 **Rituals help:**
>
> Use a start-and-end cue (e.g. 'Let's work' / 'All done')
>
> Celebrate the end with a treat or short game.
>
> 💬 **Affirmation for both of you:**
>
> We're learning. We're trying. That's enough.

CHAPTER 5

The Hard Days

There were no soft Sunday mornings with coffee and cuddles. No peaceful leash walks with smiling strangers. Most days started with pain already screaming through my joints. Sometimes I woke feeling like I had run a marathon in my sleep. My bones ached. My skin burned. Other mornings I could not even feel my feet.

But Yoshi needed movement. So, I moved.

The early weeks were chaos. She teethed on everything: my arms, pants, chair legs, her leash. Little shark teeth left trails of scratches on my already fragile skin. Some nights I cleaned tiny blood spots off my clothes and furniture, wondering if they were hers or mine.

We lived in a small apartment. No backyard. No safe space to let her run. And Yoshi had energy. So much energy. She bounced between the couch and door like a pinball. Pacing. Overstimulated even when given enough exercise and enforced naps.

So we went out. Three walks. Four. Some days five. Even when I could not catch my breath. Even when my hips buckled or migraines blurred my vision. I walked through it all: joint pain, dizziness, asthma, burning fatigue. Sometimes I cried while walking, hoping the wind would dry the tears before anyone noticed.

Still, it was not enough. She needed stimulation. Play. Training.

And training was a whole new nightmare.

Every trainer had something different to say. One accused me of making excuses. Another told me I expected too much, that she was just a baby. A third bluntly declared that she would never be a working dog, that she did not have it in her.

Their voices echoed louder than mine. And I was the one left alone with the consequences.

Meanwhile, Yoshi struggled too. Loud engines, skateboards, and sudden bangs triggered fear. People thought it was funny to rev their cars as we walked past. They did not see her bolt sideways in terror. They did not feel her trembling beside me. They did not watch her joy shrink, step by step, as phobias set in.

Being a puppy is hard. Being a puppy raised by someone living with disability and isolation in a tiny apartment is even harder.

Some days she paced with those big golden eyes that seemed to ask if there was a bigger space. And I whispered back that there was. Then I clipped on her leash anyway. Even if I had not slept in days. Even if I had eaten nothing but dry toast. Even if my body was begging for stillness.

Because that was what she needed. Because that was what love looked like when we were both struggling to survive.

We walked and walked, through tears, through pain, through fear.

And then came the night when everything changed. A night already heavy with grief. My birthday. The night when danger met us on the street and nothing felt safe again.

> **Pawnote: Caring for a Dog When You're Struggling**
>
> **Acknowledge the Hard:**
>
> Some days you just don't have it in you and that's okay. Loving your dog doesn't mean ignoring your pain or pushing past every limit.
>
> **Balance Your Needs and Theirs:**
>
> - Swap long walks for short, high-quality training sessions.
> - Use enrichment (puzzle feeders, scent games, trick training) to tire them mentally.
> - Rotate toys to keep things novel without more effort on your part.
>
> **Work With What You've Got:**
>
> If you can't leave home, create 'adventure days' indoors: hide treats around the house, teach a new cue, or set up a small obstacle course.

 REMEMBER: Dogs don't need perfection they need consistency, kindness, and connection. Even on low energy days, a few minutes of calm interaction can mean more than an hour long walk.

CHAPTER 6

The Day Everything Broke

i. Not Just Property but My Everything

It was my birthday. Lonely, miserable...
Already a battle to stay alive the whole day.

We had a walk in the morning and afternoon.
But Yoshi was still restless, bouncing off the walls with overstimulated energy.

I looked at her and sighed,
"I don't know what to do with all that, Yoshi... but let's go."

It was dark. We leashed up and headed toward the lake for what was meant to be a short, quiet walk.
I tried to stay present. Tried not to cry.

Then I heard shouting behind us, angry, fast, close.
I turned.

A man on a bicycle, hoodie up, full-face helmet, speeding toward us.
Panic lit up my nervous system.

I stepped off the footpath and onto the grass, holding Yoshi close to me.
He zoomed past, then stopped just a few metres ahead.

He turned back.
And started screaming.

Violent. Profane. Targeted.
I've dealt with people like this before. I knew the signs.
I placed Yoshi behind me, keeping my eyes on him.
She whined, unsettled.

He started pacing, hurling insults, inching closer.
I tried staying silent. It didn't help.

"What is your problem?" I finally said. "Go away."

He didn't.

"GO AWAY!" I yelled.

He threw his bike down. Charged.
I blocked the first punch. Then the second.
But in the chaos… I lost the leash.

Yoshi was gone.

I turned in time to see her sprinting straight into traffic.
Before I could run after her, he shoved me hard. From the back.
COWARDLY move.
I hit the ground. Watch strap snapped. Everything hurt.

I scrambled up, joints screaming. I was annoyed.
He threw more punches. I blocked, covered, didn't fight back. Just survived.

Then he picked up his bike and tried to throw it at me.
I stepped in. Grabbed it mid-air. Tossed it aside.

He tore off his full-face helmet and began beating me with it when I realised he was wearing a balaclava.
I blocked again. Just blocked. Always blocking.

Eventually, realising he was getting nowhere, he grabbed his bike, got back on, and started to ride away.

I pulled out my phone, desperate to get a photo.

He circled back.
Hit the phone from my hands.
And screamed:
"I HOPE YOUR DOG DIES!"

Then he vanished.

I picked my phone up and bolted.
Yelled for Yoshi. Ran across the street. Nothing.

Time slowed into terror.
She was gone.

I called the police. I tried to explain what happened.
They said I was not being calm.
They said they could not find me.
I was standing in full view, barely three hundred metres from their station.

A woman approached.
I saw everything, she said.
I asked her to speak to the police too, and she agreed.

Eventually, officers arrived and took our statements.
But when I asked about Yoshi, about my missing dog, they said she was not part of the incident. They said they could not help with that. Just property.

So can I claim that he damaged my property, since she is my assistance dog in training, I asked.
They looked confused, unprepared for the question. No, we cannot do anything about that.

Except she was not just property.
She was everything.

I had called Fab, a friend from work, while I was still waiting for the police. I told him what had happened. He and his wife arrived and helped post on social media, hoping someone might have spotted Yoshi. Then he went searching by car. And I waited. Forty minutes. Agonising, never-ending minutes.

I approached strangers, asking if they had seen her.
One snapped at me not to interrupt their walk.
Another said he would keep an eye out.

I was barely holding it together.

And then I saw a silhouette in the distance.
Two dogs. A leash.
Yoshi.

I squinted, heart racing. Yoshi.
She broke free and bolted into my arms, muddy, shaking, exhausted.

Someone had found her hiding under a bridge, not far from our usual walking path. Not the main road. Not the chaos. She had gone somewhere familiar. Somewhere safe.

Clever girl.

We walked home slowly. She did not want to be carried.

It was as if she was saying, we can do this, together.

I gripped her leash tight. I could not risk letting go again. Not now. Not ever.

At home, I gently cleaned her off.

No proper bath, just a warm rinse, enough to wash away the grime without adding more stress.

She had been through enough.

Her leash was torn, her poop bag shredded.
None of it mattered.

That night we curled up together, sore and silent.

ii. Aftermath

That night, sleep came in bursts.
Every ache in my body screamed.
Bruises bloomed across my arms, ribs, and wrists.
The next morning, I took photos.
Sent them to the police.
Evidence.

They called me back later.
"He's a known offender," they said.
"Maybe he'll lie low for a while after this."

That wasn't comfort.

Yoshi and Me

That was failure.

Why was he still out there in the first place?

After that day, my PTSD got worse.
Something in me already cracked, fractured deeper.

I didn't know who that man was.
But he knew me.
Called me by name.
Screamed it like he meant it.

And just like that, the world became sharper.
Louder.
Darker.

I flinched at sudden sounds.
Scanned every cyclist.
Every hooded figure.

I didn't want to go outside anymore.

But I did.
Because of Yoshi.

She needed walks.
She needed movement.
She needed some thread of normalcy.
And maybe… so did I.

But she had changed too.

She no longer bounced toward the door.
No more happy tail wags at the sound of keys.

Now, she flinched when engines roared.
Skirted away from trucks.
Paused at loud voices, ears back, eyes wide.

We started avoiding the intersection altogether.
Didn't go far from home.
Just short loops, safe, familiar ones.

When we got too close to that corner, she'd slow her steps.
Not walking ahead, not pulling forward
But gently tugging to the side.
As if she were saying,
'Let's not go there. Let's be safe. Please.'

She remembered.
And she was trying to protect us both.
Even if she didn't understand why.

We mirrored each other's fears.
Startled at the same noises.
Tensed at the same shadows.

Still, we walked.

I started tethering her to me with a second lead, looped across my body.
Not because I thought she'd run again,
but because I couldn't trust the world not to break us.

And, more painfully,
I couldn't trust myself.
Not to fail her again.

But she never blamed me.

Yoshi and Me

She stayed close.
Watched me carefully.
Moved with me.

She responded before I could even name the emotion rising in me.
Anticipated my panic.
Grounded my spirals.

She wasn't waiting to be trained.
She was already becoming my assistance dog.

In the way she read my silence.
In the way she gently guided me away from fear.
In the way she pressed her body against mine at night, trying to hold my broken pieces together.

We didn't just survive that day.
We survived the days after.
The dread.
The freezing panic at the thought of leaving home.
The exhaustion of being on constant alert.

We're still walking.
Still healing.
Side by side.

That night didn't break us. But it cracked open something deeper. The need for healing that we couldn't do alone.

> 🐾 **Pawnote**
>
> **Crisis Plans and What You Can Prepare**
>
> **Emergency prep with a dog:**
>
> - Use two connection points: leash + backup tether to belt or chest harness
> - Practice an 'emergency stay' cue (e.g. stop and drop)
> - Carry Bluetooth Tag or GPS on the collar if possible
> - Teach your dog to return to a 'home base' spot or car if startled
>
> **After the fact:**
>
> - Take pictures of injuries.
> - File reports, even if it feels pointless (paper trails matter)
> - Ask a friend to help post in lost/found dog groups—have a template ready to go
>
> **Emotionally** Prepare for grief, confusion, PTSD triggers. Have support lined up if you can.

CHAPTER 7

Finding our Team

Finding a trainer who truly sees both the dog and the human behind them?

That's rare.

That's Tamika.

No judgment. No rigid formulas. No "fix your dog in five easy steps" kind of talk.

Just guidance. Real, gentle, trauma-informed guidance.

We weren't handed a cookie-cutter training plan. We weren't told what we were doing wrong.

We were seen as a team. A unique one. A bruised one. A determined one. Still standing, even if a little shaky.

Still trying.

We were already speaking to someone who mentioned Tamika. It was shortly after the attack.

I could barely string thoughts together, let alone speak in full sentences. So I sent her a short, panicked text.

"Something happened. Should we stay home? Or go out and face it… desensitise?"

Her call came just as I was about to leash Yoshi up and push through the fear.

But her voice stopped me.

"No… not today," she said gently. "Stay home. Or go somewhere safe, like the members' dog field if you need to move. Don't push yourselves."

I don't remember the rest of the conversation. I just remember feeling a crack of space open in my chest.

Relief.

Permission.

And then she said something no one else had said.

"I'll come see you. The day after next."

In those two days, we breathed a little easier.

We didn't train. We didn't push. We just existed.

We spent time at the members' dog field, tucked away in the fenced area, just the two of us. Not running or playing, not really. Just staying close. I was sore from the bruises. Tired in every way. And Yoshi? She didn't need fetch or fun. She just wanted to be near me. To sit close.

It was quiet. No pressure. No noise. Just healing, in our own quiet, fumbling way.

Knowing someone was coming. Not just to help with the puppy problems. But to help with us.

With the trauma. The overwhelm. The weird grey area between 'owner' and 'disabled handler' that so few people understand.

She was coming to see the whole picture.

Not just the leash reactive moments, the overexcitement, the chewing or pulling.
But the fear behind it.
The panic.
The heartbreak.
The will to keep going when everything says stop.

Tamika stepped inside, calm and grounded, carrying a small gift bag in one hand. We had not even opened it yet, and Yoshi did not care about what was in the bag. She cared about the person holding it.

Tamika entered her play pen crouched down gently, not saying much, just offering her presence. Yoshi stepped forward slowly at first, sniffing the air, tail slightly raised but unsure. Her tail twitched once, then again, then it started to wag with rhythm, wide and happy.

And then she burst. She lit up with joy, wiggling her whole body, tail sweeping like a fan. She leaned in hard, paws on Tamika's knees, licking her face, pressing close like she had just found her favourite person in the world.

Tamika laughed and welcomed it without hesitation. She did not push her back, did not redirect her, did not tell her to settle. She just let her be.

It was the happiest I had seen Yoshi in weeks.
She was all over Tamika like sunshine, joyful, trusting, alive.
I stood back, watching my dog, who had been so shaken and so guarded, absolutely light up for this one human.
And in that moment, I did not feel so alone anymore either.

Tamika sat on the floor with us. She let Yoshi sniff, watch, and approach in her own time, even chewed on her sunglasses.

She listened to everything I said.
She asked thoughtful questions.
She did not flinch at hard answers.

There was no notebook and stopwatch, no performance pressure.
Just care.
Just kindness.
Just curiosity.

She saw a struggling puppy and a struggling human and chose not to fix either.
She chose to support both.

And it was the first time I felt like maybe we were not failing.
Maybe we were just still becoming.

Training with Tamika was not easy.
It still is not.
There were tears.
There were breakthroughs.
There were toys hidden in strange places and moments where neither of us knew what we were doing.
There were days when Yoshi did brilliant things and I forgot to celebrate.
Days when I cried after Tamika left because I realised just how much pressure I was carrying.

But there was always progress.
Not just in the tasks.
In the trust.
Every week, we grew stronger.
Not just Yoshi's training, but mine too.
My confidence.

My timing.
My ability to read her subtle cues before they turned into meltdowns.

Tamika celebrated the small wins.
She helped reframe the bad days.
She reminded me again and again that this is a marathon, not a test.
That we were already doing it.
Just by showing up.
Just by trying again.

I watched Yoshi's eyes light up as if someone had just said treat time, always buzzing with excitement.
Her tail wagged so hard it looked like a helicopter about to take off.
You could almost hear her thinking, what is next, what is the mission, when do we get snacks.

She definitely felt safe around Tamika. Like she was saying, this human is cool, I like her.
She trusted Tamika.
And slowly, I started to trust too, which honestly felt like a miracle after all the chaos.

That is what Tamika gave us.
Not just training.
Not just fancy tricks.
But belief.

And a proper tag team partnership, like Batman and Robin but with more fur and fewer gadgets.

And through it all, Yoshi kept showing me what she was already capable of. Sometimes long before I even asked.

Finding our Team

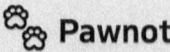 **Pawnote**

What to Look for in a Trainer Green flags:

- Listens to your story without jumping to conclusions
- Understands invisible illness and trauma-informed support
- Adapts plans based on both *you* and the dog

Red flags:

- Forces eye contact or obedience over consent
- Blames you or your disability for setbacks
- Won't explain techniques in plain language
- Bad mouth every other trainers.

Ask during consults:

- 'How do you structure sessions for people with fatigue or trauma?'

 BONUS TIP: The right trainer leaves you feeling hopeful, not defeated. If you walk away from a session feeling worse than when you arrived, it is a sign that you are not in the right room. Do not be afraid to explore other options. A great trainer will not only understand but will gladly point you toward someone who might be a better fit.

CHAPTER 8

Tasks She Taught Herself: Because She's Magic

Yoshi has this incredible superpower: she just knows. Before I even realise what I need, she is already on it. Like some kind of furry psychic, but way cuter and with better intuition than any self-help book I have ever read.

For example, she began alerting me to pain before I could even say ouch. She blocks people when my anxiety spikes in noisy crowds, turning herself into a four legged, wagging bodyguard. And when I cannot breathe, she does not just sit there looking worried. She plops herself right on my chest as if to say, hey, calm down human, I got you, chill.

Here is the thing: I did not teach her any of this. She just did it, like magic. I took those amazing instincts, gave them names, reinforced the behaviours, but that initial spark, the real magic, that was all Yoshi.

She is not a tool on a leash. She is my teammate. And honestly, I am convinced there is some kind of wizardry going on in those paws.

Buffering: The Invisible Bubble Creator

You know those moments when you are stuck in a crowd and you want to yell for people to back off because you are anxious, but instead you just try to disappear into your own shadow? That was me before Yoshi.

Now Yoshi is my personal bouncer. When things get noisy and packed, in shopping centres, community events, basically anywhere humans like to swarm, she spins around me she moves like a furry little bodyguard, creating an invisible Do Not Disturb bubble. I say Circle and she moves from heel at my left, stepping into a backward circle around my legs until she completes the full three hundred and sixty, brushing against me the whole time as if she is saying no, you shall not pass. And she does it all with the cutest possible face...

Here is the funny part. Yoshi is still scared of loud places and big crowds. Malls are not her favourite. She tucks herself close, ears pinned back, but she is determined. She wants to be with me, to help me through it. Even if that help looks like this: she tells me, with all the urgency she can muster in her doggy way, quick, grab that thing you need. Then she patiently waits for me to pick it up like a good shopping assistant before hustling me all the way to the checkout and back into the car, like we are on some kind of speed shopping mission.

Yoshi might be a little scared, but she is brave when it counts. And honestly, I do not know who is helping who more.

Deep Pressure Therapy: The Lap Blanket That Moves

When depression or chronic pain crash the party, sometimes I just need a little comforting weight on me. That is when Yoshi turns into a living, breathing weighted blanket, only way cuter and with more personality.

If I am on the floor or sitting on the couch, she gently lays her front paws over my legs, not her whole body because she knows she is a hefty gal, and stays perfectly still as if she is meditating on how awesome I am. If I am sitting, she will plop her chin on my lap, giving me the look that only a dog can pull off, the I am here for you look.

It is like having a warm, calming presence that says, you have got this buddy. Honestly, it is better than any human cuddle I have ever had.

The Bed Surprise: Defying the Rules of Comfort

Yoshi is picky about beds. She has better beds than I do, with fancy blankets and her own little spot on the floor that is definitely cooler and way bigger than my tiny warm bed. So it is kind of a miracle when she actually climbs up onto my bed at all.

But on those nights when my pain is flaring up or when nightmares sneak in, she hops up as if she is saying, alright human, this is an emergency cuddle situation. She squeezes herself into our small space, despite the obvious too warm and too small logic, and settles in close to make sure I am okay.

Sometimes, when I am writhing in pain or twisting in a nightmare, she nudges me gently or rests her head on me like a furry little lifeline. It is her way of interrupting the bad vibes and saying, I am right here, you are not alone.

It is hard to explain how much that means. How this big, warm, somewhat bossy ball of fur can bring calm just by being there.

Behavioural Interruption: The Nose Boop Ninja (and Paw-sitive Persuader)

Sometimes my brain decides to throw a tantrum. Breath holding, leg shaking, finger tapping. The full stuck in my own head routine.

Yoshi has a secret weapon: the Nose Boop. She gently boops my leg like a tiny, persistent alarm clock saying, hey, focus, you are missing the plot here.

I will admit, sometimes I am so zoned out that I ignore her. But Yoshi does not take rejection lightly. After three polite nose boops she moves to what I call paw-sitive persuasion. This means a dramatic leap onto my lap with her paws firmly planted on my chest, staring straight into my soul as if to say, listen here human, I am not just a cute fluffball, I am your emotional lifeline. You will listen to me right now.

Her eyes are so intense you would think she was auditioning for a role in a soap opera. And honestly, it works. How can I stay stuck in my head when she is giving me that much paw-sitive pressure?

The Self Harm Interrupter (The Ultimate Guardian)

This is where Yoshi's magic really blows my mind. When my emotions spiral and I am on the edge of hurting myself, she is right there. No hesitation. She climbs onto me, making me sit down, then rests her paws and chin on my arms like a gentle furry jailer saying, not today.

She has this look, half stern and half loving, that says, you are not alone. I am here to stop you, but also to hold you. It is the kind of support that cannot be put into words.

She even keeps tabs on my punching bag sessions. If I start hitting too hard or getting sloppy, she interrupts with her special enough look, then gets me down on the ground and lays over me as if to say, come on, get a grip. We are in this together.

Yoshi's endless patience and quiet strength make her the best therapist I never knew I needed.

Every Day Is a Team Effort

Since I got her, I have woken up every day trying to find new ways to survive with her by my side. It is like having a furry life coach who never sleeps, never judges, and always insists on helping whether I ask for it or not.

Some days she is my motivational speaker. Other days she is my personal space creator. On the toughest days, she is the warm fuzzy anchor that keeps me grounded. Together, we figure out the little hacks and tricks that help me get through the chaos.

Surviving with Yoshi is not just about managing symptoms or tasks. It is about partnership, trust, and a kind of magic you cannot bottle. And honestly, it is the best kind of magic there is.

Yoshi is not just a dog. She is my partner in crime, my emotional bodyguard, my fuzzy superhero. She pulls me back from the edge, breaks through my silence, and reminds me I am not alone. The world may not always see her, but I do. And that is enough.

 Pawnote

When Dogs Do the Teaching Natural behaviours to watch for:

- Staring at you when your breathing changes? That's a prompt.
- Moving closer when you dissociate? That's anchoring.
- Booping or pawing when you're still for too long? That's interruption.

What you can do:

- Name the behaviour (e.g. 'Focus', 'Alert', 'Nudge').
- Reward consistently. Yes, even for the 15th boop in a row.
- Pair the behaviour with a cue when you're *not* in crisis.

 REMEMBER: You don't have to invent all the tasks. Sometimes the best ones are discovered, not taught.

CHAPTER 9

Rewriting My Days Around Her Paws

Invisible disabilities have a strange kind of presence. They take up space, even when no one else sees them. It feels like being a ghost with a pulse, moving through the world unnoticed until you stumble, break, or collapse.

If you are not in a wheelchair, if you are not wearing a cast, if you can smile while you are falling apart inside, then surely you are fine. Right?
'Can't be that bad.'
'You look normal.'
'You don't seem disabled.'
The classics. The greatest hits from people who believe pain only counts if it is visible.

But here is the truth: just because you cannot see it does not mean it is not heavy. It does not mean it does not hurt. The absence of bandages or crutches does not make the battles any less real.

Yoshi does not need to see my trauma to understand it. She knows when I have not slept, when my chest tightens, when my hands tremble, when my whole body hums with pain and panic. She validates the battles I fight in silence, the ones no one else notices unless I fall apart.

She knows me without explanation. No doctor's note. No paperwork. No justification.

And still, the world does not always catch up. People stare when she performs a task. They whisper when I kneel to give her a cue or lean into her for grounding. They side-eye when I leave early or skip small talk. They assume I am faking, exaggerating, 'using a cute dog' for special treatment.

They do not see the nights I do not sleep. The mornings I cannot move. The mental gymnastics it takes to be in public at all, the pacing, the bargaining, the careful planning for an escape route if things go wrong.

But this is not about them. It is about us. About Yoshi and me.

Before Yoshi, my days had no shape. Mornings were battles. Afternoons were fog. Nights were dreadful. I was not really living, I was surviving. Pain. Flashbacks. Exhaustion. Guilt. An endless loop with no off button.

Now my mornings start with a nose nudge. A warm reminder that someone depends on me. That I matter. That I am needed.

We train. We walk. We play. But mostly, we exist together with purpose.

Every activity is a choice. A small act of rebellion against the voice that says, 'you cannot'. Every task is a step toward independence.

Yoshi does not just support me. She structures me. She senses panic before it peaks. If I dissociate, she interrupts gently but firmly. If I freeze, she gets me moving. If I sink into the fog, she anchors me. She does not demand I do everything, but she makes sure I do not do nothing. She gives my days rhythm.

It is not about strict routines or colour-coded schedules. It is about our rhythm.

Rewriting My Days Around Her Paws

Some days, the beat is steady. Other days, it is messy and off-key. But it is ours. And slowly, with every nudge, every boop, every paw pressed to my chest, she helps rebuild my life.

One quiet, patient pawprint at a time.

Invisible disabilities are real. And we take up space, with or without permission. Sometimes that space is a queue at the shops. Sometimes it is a park bench where I catch my breath. Sometimes it is just the patch of carpet where Yoshi and I curl up together, reminding each other that we are enough.

> 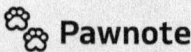 **Pawnote**
>
> **Tiny Wins and Everyday Tools**
>
> Some days, success is just getting out of bed before lunch. Other days, it is making it through the shops without bolting. Wins do not always look like medals. Sometimes they look like staying in a queue, gripping your dog's fur to stay grounded, or leaving the house even if you only make it to the letterbox.
>
> Stack enough of those little victories, and you have got a parade, even if it is just you, a coffee, and a dog who thinks they are the mayor. Along the way, there are simple skills you can teach your dog that make those wins easier to reach:
>
> **Blocking (crowd control):** Teach 'middle' or 'side' using body cues. Reinforce when they step between you and others. Helpful in queues, tight spaces, or whenever you need personal space protected.

- **Grounding (emotional weight training):** Train your dog to lean or rest their head on your lap. Practise first during calm moments, then add a cue like 'touch', 'lap', or 'deep'. The gentle pressure reminds your body you are safe.

- **Bravery in action:** Celebrate their attempts, even when imperfect. And remember, they need protection too. If they are scared, they need comfort and recovery time as much as we do.

 TIP: Confidence is not forced. It grows with trust and consistency, layered slowly like pawprints forming a trail.

CHAPTER 10

Paperwork, Perfection, and Puppyhood

They never tell you this part. That the journey of training your own assistance dog isn't just about trust, connection, or the hours of work you put in together. It's also about paperwork. Never-ending, soul-draining, spirit-crushing paperwork.

Everything has to be logged for assistance dog proof of training. Every training session. Every cue practiced. Every outing. Every behaviour. Every correction. Every win. Every stumble. There is always a form, a template, a logbook, a spreadsheet. And somewhere, someone is expecting to see progress. Every few months, someone pops up and asks for evidence. Proof that we are achieving. That we are on track. That we are measuring up.

Sometimes it feels like we are being graded like a high school science project. But the truth is, keeping records matters. The logbooks show that the work is real. They remind me how far we have come when the days feel heavy. And when someone questions us, they are the proof that Yoshi is not just a pet but a trained partner who has earned her place by my side.

Paperwork, Perfection, and Puppyhood

Yoshi is expected to be flawless. Every fear she has. She must conquer it. Every reaction? Must be perfect. Every cue? Followed instantly, without hesitation, like a little robot coded to someone else's ideal of perfection. And if she doesn't? It's not the system that needs adjusting. It's us.

But here's the thing: no one seems to want to hear she's not a machine. She's not a perfect code or programmable unit. She's a living, breathing being. A puppy My puppy.

People scoff when I say dogs are like toddlers, but it is true. Training a dog is like parenting a stubborn, hilarious, emotionally honest three-year-old who gets distracted by butterflies and is deeply offended by loud trucks. You cannot just slap on a behaviour template and expect it to work. Learning does not look the same for every dog or every handler. And yet we are told to force them all through the same narrow training funnel.

Then came the realisation that hit like a brick to the gut: all assistance dogs must pass a Public Access Test. And not just once. Every single year. That is not optional. That is mandatory.

And who pays for that? Who pays for the training, the gear, the assessments, the travel, the time off work if you can work at all, and the annual retesting?

I am someone who struggles to work consistently because of chronic illness and disability. I cannot afford a daily coffee, let alone hundreds or even thousands of dollars each year just to tick the right boxes for a dog that already does more for me than most humans ever have. So how?

The NDIS launched a taskforce to investigate assistance animal supports. And honestly, let us not even talk about it… They asked for our input, how lovely. But while they collect our thoughts and run consultations, we are drowning in expenses and red tape, trying to keep up with standards that do not make room for the realities we live in.

We are not just raising dogs. We are raising dogs while battling a system that constantly asks for more but rarely gives back.

One form. Then another. Then a test. Then a new requirement. Then a reassessment. Then another justification.

It never ends. And honestly? I am tired.

This is not just about training a dog. It is about trying to keep your head above water in a system that measures worth in boxes ticked and behaviours performed, where love, loyalty, and lifesaving support do not count unless they come with a signed certificate and a laminated handler ID.

But Yoshi does not care about paperwork.

She sees me in pain and nudges me. She senses when I am shutting down and licks my hand. She blocks strangers from coming too close when I am overwhelmed. She is already doing the job.

The only thing imperfect is the system trying to deny it.

And still, some blamed the dog, when the real problem was never her.

Paperwork, Perfection, and Puppyhood

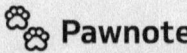 **Pawnote**

The Admin Side of Assistance Dog Life

What to track:

- Training logs (brief entries: task, location, behaviour).
- Notes on public access practice.
- Progress videos (a lifesaver for assessments).

How often?

- Weekly is ideal.
- Monthly is still helpful.
- Anything is better than 'I will remember it later'.

 PRO TIP:

- Use voice memos if writing is difficult.
- Create folders by topic: 'Tasks', 'Access Practice', 'Health', 'Vet'.

PAT (Public Access Test) basics:

- Dog must always be under control.
- Calm in public.
- Ignoring food and people distractions.
- Performing tasks relevant to your disability.

> **Reality check:**
>
> Passing once does not mean the stress ends. But it does give you peace of mind and legal ground to stand on. In Australia, you currently need to retest every 12 months. Consultations are underway and hopefully the law changes. It is not cheap.

CHAPTER 11

People Are the Problem

Here's a hard truth: Sometimes, the most exhausting part of having disabilities... Is not the disability.

It's the people.

The stares. The whispers. The unsolicited comments. The strangers who stop and quiz me like I'm failing a pop quiz on my own life. The ones who see Yoshi beside me and feel the sudden urge to inspect, interrogate, or invalidate.

It's the disbelief that follows me everywhere. Like I owe an explanation for parking in a disabled space, for using an accessible bathroom, for existing in public while looking fine. Permit on the dash. Assistance dog by my side. And still, some people assume I'm faking it.

As if looking young or standing upright or cracking a joke means I can't be struggling. As if disability has to be dramatic and visible to count.

The Side-Eye Olympics

Let's talk about those moments, the little ones that build up over time. I pull into a disabled parking space and notice someone slowing down to see if I 'look disabled enough'.
Leaving the disabled toilet and being met with a sharp glance or a disapproving shake of the head.
No words exchanged. Just judgment.

Sometimes there are words.
'That's for people who need it.'
'You look fine to me.'
'You shouldn't be using that.'

They do not see what Yoshi sees.
They do not see the pain that makes standing for too long unbearable.
The panic that makes queues feel like tightropes over cliffs.
The dissociation that makes a safe, private toilet space more than a convenience: it is a lifeline.

And in those moments when someone decides I do not deserve support because I do not fit their idea of what disability looks like, it stings. No matter how used to it I get.

Yoshi Doesn't Ask for Proof

That's the thing. Yoshi does not need proof. She does not need a medical file or a label. She does not care what I look like or whether other people believe me.

She sees what others do not. The subtle shifts. The tension in my hands. The glazed look in my eyes when I start to slip away. She moves in. Noses me. Grounds me. Reminds me I am here, I am safe, and I am not alone. That is the only validation I need.

Yoshi and Me

It's Not My Job to Convince You

I did not leave my house today to be your learning experience. I am not a walking FAQ, and I do not come with a 'Justify My Existence' button. I came out to live. To function. To survive. Just like anyone else.

But here we go again… The stares. The head tilts. The oh-so-predictable: 'Are you training that dog for someone else?' 'Why do you need an assistance dog, if you don't mind me asking?'

Actually, I do mind. No, I am not training her for anyone else. Yes, Yoshi is my assistance dog. Yes, I need her. And no, you do not get to ask.

Because I do not look 'disabled enough,' you are taken aback. Because I dare to exist without limping, without a cane, without fitting your checklist.

But let me spell it out. Disability does not have a dress code. Needing help does not come with a neon sign.

Yoshi is not here for fun. She is not a pet, she is a partner. She catches me before I crash. She grounds me when my world spins out. She is trained to help with things you cannot see, but that does not make them any less real.

She is my lifeline. My furry anchor. She is the reason I can go out into a world that too often tries to break me.

So, unless you are offering her a treat or me some peace, keep your questions on a leash.

I am not here to entertain your doubt. I am not your feel-good inspiration. And I am not doing this for your comfort.

You want me to explain?
Sure. But I will need a coffee, a comfy chair, and an hourly rate, because walking you through your own ignorance is not in my free time budget.

And honestly?
I would rather be spending that energy on literally anything else, including dodging unsolicited advice, dodgy looks, and dodging people like you.

We Belong Here, Too

Yoshi and I take up space.
In shops. In queues. In car parks and public bathrooms.
In waiting rooms. On hospital floors.
In all the places marked 'accessible' but only if your disability looks like the brochure.

We belong there.
Even if we do not fit the neat, clinical boxes people expect.
Even if our presence shatters someone's picture-perfect idea of what 'disabled' is supposed to look like.
Even if our calm, capable dog causes panic: not because of what she does, but because she dares to be there.

I get it. Some people are afraid of dogs.
Some people are afraid of crickets, balloons, or worms, too.
Phobias are real.
But so are we.

So when we walk into a hospital and the nurse screams like we have wheeled in a live grenade, or someone yelps and leaps three feet in the shops because we dared to shuffle past them, that is not okay.

It is not just awkward.
It is painful.
It is jarring.
It is terrifying: for me, and for Yoshi.

She is working. I am just trying to exist.
We should not have to brace ourselves every time we move an inch.

And honestly?
We are not sure who is scarier in those moments: us, or the people shrieking at the sight of a dog calmly doing her job.

We are not a threat.
We are not here to entertain, inspire, or educate you on command.
We are just trying to live in a world that often forgets we belong in it.

But we do.
With paws, with purpose, with quiet strength and unshakable love.
We belong here just as much as anyone else.

So please, take a deep breath.
Maybe even two.
And remember:
Yoshi and I are not the problem.
People's fear, assumptions, and volume control?
That is another story.

Even places that claimed to care, weren't always safe. Especially the one I worked at.

> 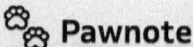 **Pawnote**
>
> **Dealing with Doubt, Stares, and Skeptics**
>
> **But you don't look disabled' Survival Kit:**
>
> - Practice short, neutral replies: 'We're working', 'She's task-trained', 'I have a disability'
> - Wear a vest with 'Assistance Dog' or 'Do Not Distract' on it
> - Bring cards to hand out to nosy people if you are too tired to speak.

Set boundaries early:

- 'Please don't pat her, she's working.'
- 'She's here for medical support.'
- 'I'm not comfortable answering personal questions.'

Emotional energy-saving mode:

- You don't owe anyone a story.
- You don't need to 'look' disabled.
- You don't need to convince anyone of your reality.

 PRO-TIP: If someone crosses a line? Walk away. They're not your audience. Your dog is.

CHAPTER 12

Yoshi Wasn't the Problem

I took the job because I believed in the mission. It was not just a job. It was a place I thought would understand what it meant to live with disability. To accommodate. To include. To care.

At first, they told me I could work flexibly, wherever suited me best. That mattered. I had already disclosed everything: PTSD, chronic illness, anxiety, autism, ADHD. And Yoshi, my assistance dog in training who was coming. We came as a package deal. That was the agreement. I then got Yoshi.

But when the new operations committee came in, things changed quickly. Suddenly, the flexibility disappeared. I was expected to work all my hours on-site. Never mind that the building had no proper air conditioning. That the admin offices had dirty, decades-old carpets, broken furniture, cables dangling like spider webs, paper stacked everywhere that could supply hours of bonfire. Never mind that I had respiratory conditions and Yoshi's paw had already been caught in frayed carpet threads. Never mind that there was no safe place for her, no space designated, no thought given.

They said, 'You need to be here if you want to keep the job.' So I went in. And I brought Yoshi with me, because I had to. Because I could not function without her. Because she does real disability work: grounding me, interrupting panic attacks, shielding me in crowded spaces, alerting me to danger when I dissociate. She is my reason to survive the day.

But instead of accommodations, I got complaints. Jokes about Yoshi stinking up the office, when she had just been bathed. Rude comments about hiring someone in the organisation just to wash her. Mockery over having a 'special' dog and the nerve to make rules, such as asking people not to pat her while she was working.

They were thrilled to meet her when she was a puppy. But the moment I asked for boundaries, it rubbed some of them the wrong way. She became a nuisance. I became difficult.

What they did not see, what they refused to see, was that Yoshi kept me going in that environment. She was the reason I did not lose it. She was the reason I did not walk out after yet another unpaid month. Or when they gave me five people's worth of work and paid me less than half of one. Or when they accused me of non-compliance because I did not magically fix every problem overnight.

They made me prove my hours, prove my work, prove my worth. I provided timesheets. Detailed reports. Calls. Emails. Updates. Logs. Meetings. Everything short of live streaming myself 24/7. Still, it was never enough.

They said, 'You did not attend video conferences,' but I had proof colleagues were told to email or call. I even set up social hours so colleagues could talk if they wanted. None of them came. Then they said, 'You did not get permission for this,' even when I did. Then they said, 'You are not allowed to bring your dog.'

They raised their voices. They talked over me. One said, 'It is not in your contract.' Another mumbled something supportive and then did nothing.

They knew about my disabilities. I disclosed them when I started: PTSD, anxiety, trauma. The flexible work arrangement was essential, and they agreed to it at the beginning. But when it came time to actually uphold that agreement, suddenly I was the burden. The problem. The one asking too much.

There were rooms I could have used. They were available. But I was not allowed. And even when I found grants to fix the place, the upgrades only went to the reception area, not the offices we actually worked in. We still had no ventilation, safety hazards everywhere, and office bullies making my life hell.

And still, I stayed.
Because I believed. Because I wanted to believe.

But eventually, I could not anymore.
Yoshi deserved better. I deserved better.

I walked away from a job I gave everything to. All the extra hours. All the unpaid time. All the patience I didn't have. I was exhausted. Crushed.

And then came the silence.
The job market did not want me either.
Not when I needed flexibility. Not when I mentioned an assistance dog. I did not even need her every day, just the ability to bring her when necessary, or to work from home if I was not doing well.

But no.
More than 1,000 applications.
Fewer than 50 interviews.
Most disappeared the second I mentioned anything resembling accommodations for disabilities. Even when I was willing to discuss what is possible or what is not. It felt like everything was not.

Even disability-specific recruitment agencies could not help. They did not want to deal with the dog. Or they told me to leave her out of my applications, pretend I did not need her, for now. Hide the truth for now.

I have two degrees. Diplomas. Certifications. Experience in multiple industries. I have started businesses. I have built teams. I have saved organisations.
But now, I am either too much or not enough.
Too qualified. Not qualified enough. Never just right.

And yes, people ask, 'Why are you being picky?'
As if compromising medical needs for less pay is an achievement.
As if I have not been compromising for years already.

I do not have a partner. I do not have family to fall back on. It is just me and Yoshi. And while I would love to say her selling paw pics online could help, I do not think that is going to cover the rent.

We get those funny people who ask why I cannot get a partner as well. As if I could just pick one out from the store for free.

We have cut back on everything we can. We live on the bare minimum. And still, the world tells us we are asking for too much.
But we are not.
We are just asking for a chance.

Somehow, even in the exhaustion, we found a way to keep showing up, for each other.

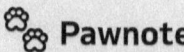 **Pawnote**

When Workplaces Do Not Work for You (or Your Dog)

Know your rights:

- The DDA protects your right to bring an assistance dog if they meet the criteria
- Reasonable adjustments must be considered, especially for disability-related supports

What to document:

- Initial agreements (emails, texts, contracts)
- Requests for accommodations
- Rejections and responses

Signs it is not working:

- Constant resistance to the dog
- No support for your well-being
- Dismissal of your condition or needs

If you must advocate:

- Stay calm, document everything, bring a support person
- Use terms like 'reasonable adjustments', 'disability access', and 'duty of care'.

 REMINDER: If it feels unsafe, you are not failing for walking away. You are protecting your energy, for you and for your dog.

CHAPTER 13

The Shape of Resilience

Resilience does not always look like grand gestures. Sometimes it looks like two exhausted souls showing up, quietly, again and again, even when it feels like everything is falling apart.

Our trainer finally had time. Amidst the chaos of her own life and emergencies, she carved out space for us. I do not know how she did it. But she did. She showed up. She did not just show up physically; she was present. Generous with her time, patient but precise, and a stickler for getting it right.

She never said it outright at that point in time, but I knew her heart was in it. She wanted Yoshi to be the best version of herself. Not just for the sake of passing some test, but because she believed in her. In us.

She spread the sessions over a few days. There was no pressure. Just the rhythm of, 'Wake up, let us meet here. We will tick off a few things today, see how she does, then come back tomorrow.'

But life does not pause when training ramps up. By day two, both Yoshi and I were feeling off. Run down. My body was aching in that way I knew too well, the kind that warns of a flare-up coming. And Yoshi, she started vomiting. That night, she threw up again. Something was wrong.

The next morning, I asked her: "Do you need to stay home today? Or can we do this thing?" She looked at me with those soft, tired eyes. And then, with the gentlest confidence, she picked the 'go do this' hand. She still wanted to work.

I triple-checked. This was not something I would ever force her into. We have developed this communication method between us: I present two closed fists, 'yes' or 'no', 'go to work' or 'stay home', and she picks. Sometimes she pauses, and if she does not like the options, she will not choose until I give her one that sits better with her. She is that smart.

But this time, she was sure. She wanted to go. So we did. We tried to keep it simple and make it short.

After the session, I rushed her to the vet. They decided to keep her in for tests. I told them to call me when they had news. A little later, they said she might need to stay the night. I asked if she could come home instead. If she was not in critical condition, she would be more comfortable with me. They said they would let me know.

But I could not wait around. I had to work. Because adult life does not pause for emergencies, not even the heartbreaking ones.

We paid someone to pick her up and bring her home, because I could not get there in time. I called the vet, paid over the phone, and then went straight into work. Heart pounding. Head spinning. Trying to act normal while my mind was still stuck in that vet's office, next to her.

The Shape of Resilience

When I finally made it home, she crawled into my lap like nothing had happened. Like the earth hadn't tilted. Like we weren't both quietly breaking.

The next morning, we woke up exhausted—but we went to our test anyway. Like it was just another day.

And you know what? We did it. We're officially recognised as an Assistance Dog in Training team!

We ticked every last box.

Right after that we decided to celebrate, we packed up a foldable pool, some water bottles, and treats, and headed to our member's dog field. I filled the pool while she watched, tail wagging in anticipation. And when it was full, she leapt in like it was the ocean itself. Jumped out. Zoomies. Back in. Splash. Splash. Zoom. Collapse. Soak. Wiggle. Smile.

That field became our sanctuary.

That little blue foldable pool? Our reward.

That moment of joy? Our resilience, made visible.

We don't talk enough about what it takes to get through a week like that. The decisions. The sacrifices. The quiet bravery of pushing through sickness and stress. The cost of pretending everything's fine so you can function in a system that never stops demanding.

But that's resilience.

It's not perfection. It's not smiling through everything.

It's the quiet decision to show up anyway. It's your dog picking your hand, even when she's tired. It's the joy in the smallest pool the day after you both barely made it.

It's knowing that somehow, you both kept going.

And that's more than enough.

And just when I thought we might have nothing left, Yoshi reminded me: joy is still possible.

🐾 Pawnote

- **What Resilience *Actually* Looks Like**

Signs you're doing enough:

- You're still trying, even on the hard days.
- You adjust the plan when needed.
- Your dog still looks to you with trust.

Celebrate the small:

- First calm walk in a new place.
- Staying grounded in a public bathroom.
- Rebounding from a meltdown together.

Rest is part of resilience:

- Schedule rest days like training days.
- Let "doing nothing" be a valid option.
- Model emotional recovery for your dog.

Quote to remember:

Resilience isn't about never breaking. It's about learning how to glue the cracks with love.

CHAPTER 14

Yoshi's Social Life Is Better Than Mine

Yoshi has more friends than I do.
Let us just start there.

It is not even close. While I spend hours overthinking how to say 'hi' in a text, she is out there making connections with her whole body. Her tail wags are not just wags; they are full-body celebrations. She radiates joy when she sees someone she loves. And somehow, she pulls me, her autistic, introverted, socially anxious human, out into the world with her.

She takes me to meet her friends.

Besides Tamika, her dog walker, Angela is one of her favourite people on earth. Yoshi knows that when Angela comes, she is about to have the best day ever. The moment she hears, "Angela is coming," it begins. The tail starts spinning like a helicopter. She paces, squeaks, pulls at the lead to get out the door, and practically throws herself into the car as soon as Angela pulls up. That goodbye glance back at me is brief, just a flicker, as if to say, *You will be home later, right?* 'Yes, little one. I will see you tonight'.

Because of work, I cannot always take her out myself. I work late. That is why we have a dog walker in the first place. Sometimes I leave before the pick-up, and by the time I get home, she has already had her big adventure.

When I walk through the door, she is usually curled up on her bed, tired and content. I am usually just as exhausted: physically, mentally, and emotionally. Most days, I come home running on empty.

But the moment she hears me, there it is again: that same waggy, happy tail. Then comes the full-body stretch, followed by the 'I missed you so much' wiggle.

Even on the hardest days, I cannot help but hug her tight, burying my face in her fur. 'Tell me about your day', I whisper, as if she might answer. She always smells of sunshine and creek water, and her paws are still dusted with traces of wherever she has been tiny souvenirs from a world she explored without me.

She does not even lift her head at first. She just sighs in her sleep, wiped out from a day full of friends and freedom.

The walk reports and videos are my favourite thing to check after a long day at work. They never fail to make me smile:

'Yoshi made a new friend today.' 'Parkoured.' 'What is that dog even doing?' Usually paired with a chaotic photo or video that perfectly captures her being her goofy, fearless self.

It is like getting little postcards from her adventures, proof that while I am stuck in meetings and screens, she is out there living her best life.

Angela has known her since she was a tiny puppy. And we are lucky. On Angela's days off, if we are free, we sometimes might get to tag along for a walk.

And those days? Those are Yoshi's best days.

She lights up when we all walk together. She gets to show me her world. And Angela has even shared her favourite spots with us, so I can take Yoshi out on solo adventures too.

We have explored Mount Rogers, wandered Palmersville, learnt about Yarramundi, discovered new dog ovals and shady little parks tucked away like secrets, all thanks to Yoshi's people.

She even got invited to her bestie's birthday party. Katsu the Cavoodle turned one.

Apparently, when Yoshi and Katsu are together, they are chaotic joy incarnate crazy, hilarious, running nonstop, carrying sticks side by side like a pair of wild toddlers, and exploring every inch of the outdoors during their pack walks.

They do not just play. They launch. They zoom. They are somehow both adorable and a health hazard.

Yoshi's Social Life Is Better Than Mine

We have made more friends at dock diving too, dogs and humans alike. Some weekends, we meet up with Isla and Ghost.

Yes. Ghost. The dog. Facebook once told me it was 'inappropriate' to say, 'We went walking with Ghost,' but I swear, we did. He is very much alive. And very much fluffy.

Yoshi does not discriminate. She plays with blind dogs, deaf dogs, old dogs, young ones, anxious ones, and socially awkward ones, just like her human. If they want to play, she is all in.

As long as they are not rough or bossy. If they do not want to play, she politely greets them and moves on.

She has preferences, sure: dogs she clicks with, dogs she does not. But she is respectful. There is a short sprint, a quick sniff, and if she is not feeling it, she will simply do her own thing.

Sometimes she will even come over and give me that 'We are done here' look. 'Time to go, human'.

Because of Yoshi, I have met people I never would have dared to approach. I have stood in paddocks, on trails, by rivers, chatting (awkwardly) with other dog people, even laughing sometimes. I have found a community I did not know I could be part of.

She is not just my assistance dog. She is not just my support. She is my link to the world. She is the reason I keep trying to be brave.

And yes, she still has far more friends than me.

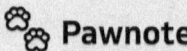 **Pawnote**

Dogs Need Community.

Enrichment beyond you:
- Walks with other dogs (solo or group).
- Sniffing trails, bushland, changing routes.
- Playdates or structured daycare (with vetting).

Finding the right dog walker:

- Ask about experience with assistance or working dogs.
- Review safety protocols, transport, handling methods.

Helpful touch:

- Ask for photo or video updates; they bring peace of mind and joy when you are stuck working.

 BONUS: Your dog's community becomes your community. People remember you because of them.

CHAPTER 15

Juggling, Joy, and Just Showing Up

Some days, it feels like we have figured it all out.
Other days, we are just juggling.
Dropping balls.
Pretending that was not the last of our sanity rolling under the couch.

We are still learning.
Still adjusting to each other.
To my body's unpredictability.
To Yoshi's ever-evolving needs.
To life, work, fatigue, fear, and finances.

But one thing never changes: **I put her first.**

If I have to be at work by 7am, I am up at 6.
Not to shower. Not to eat. Not to scroll or breathe.
But to take her out.

Juggling, Joy, and Just Showing Up

A short walk. Enough movement to start her day right.
Then we wait 45 minutes, because digestion matters, and only then do I feed her.

I grab my bag. I leave.
She watches me go.
And I miss her the moment I close the door.
I think she misses me too.

She is subtle about it most days.
But her eyes say it. Her body says it.
The wiggle, the sigh, the quiet *where have you been* sniff-down when I come home. Yes, she missed me.

If I can, I make sure her dog walker takes her out while I am gone.
If not, she waits.
And I come home exhausted, but I still clip on her lead and head out again.
Big Walk. Bigger play.
Because her day matters too.

And if money is tight, which it usually is, she still eats before I do. She does not know it, but I have had days where it was just toast for me, while she munched on allergy-friendly kibble and air-fried chicken bits I had prepped over the weekend.

I even bought a dehydrator.
Not for me.
For her.

To save money and make her treats from real chicken breast: no strange fillers, no mystery ingredients.
She loves them.
And I love that she loves them.

She earns them too.
When she blocks someone from getting too close.
When she nudges me out of a panic.
When she looks up as if to say, 'Did I do good?'

The answer is always yes.
And the treat is always ready.

Our trainer, Tamika, once said something that stuck with me: "Would you work if someone only paid you in peanuts or M&Ms?"

Nope. And neither should Yoshi.

Juggling, Joy, and Just Showing Up

She is the only reason I am alive.
So I pay her.
In food. In toys. In space. In kindness.
In every bit of energy I can spare, and then some.

Even when work is not flexible.
Even when life is not kind.
Even when I am running on fumes and fraying at the edges, I still build my life around her as much as I can.

Because she did not ask for this job.
She simply stepped into it, with loyalty, softness, and heart.
She became everything I did not know I needed.

So I do my best to give her everything she deserves.

That is why we do not just walk the same streets every day. We explore. We find new trails. Secret paths. Shady ovals tucked between suburbs. Sometimes the adventure is short and slow. Other times we wander longer than planned, chasing sunbeams or the scent of something mysterious to her but invisible to me.

We try sports too.
Dock diving. Nose work. Agility.
Not for ribbons or titles. Yoshi could not care less about trophies.

We do it for fun. For confidence. For shared laughter. For moments where we both forget the weight of the world and simply play.

We create experiences.
For her. For me. For us.
Moments of joy that are not measured in wins or progress charts. Only in tail wags, in eye contact, in freedom.

We are still figuring things out.
Still juggling.
Still dropping balls sometimes.
But we keep showing up for each other.

And honestly?
That is enough.

 Pawnote

You Are Building a Life, Not a Performance

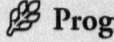 **Progress is not always measurable:**

- Not every walk needs structure
- Not every activity needs a goal
- Joy is reason enough

Training is more than tasks:

- It is saying *yes* to adventure

- It is making space for mess
- It is following your dog's lead, even off the script

♥ **You are doing more than you think:**

- Making treats from scratch
- Rearranging your life for their well-being
- Giving them the freedom to simply be a dog

 REMINDER: Your dog does not need you to be perfect.
They need you to be present.
And that is everything.

CHAPTER 16

When People Hurt, She Heals

Some people can be cruel. They smile to your face and throw rocks the moment you turn your back. Not real rocks, perhaps, but words sharp enough to cut.

Accusations. Assumptions. Condescending tones.
And the worst part?
They still expect you to thank them for it.

Some days it feels like I am walking through life with a target on my chest and no armour left. Surgeries. Appointments. Paperwork. Work shifts I cannot afford to miss. All while pretending I have someone waiting at home.

Because if I tell the truth, that I do not, I get denied help.
After my third surgery in seven months, the hospital made it clear: 'No support person, no surgery.'

As if everyone has someone.
As if loneliness is not a valid reason to need care.
As if I do not exist in the margins of their rules.

So, I lied.
I said I had someone to pick me up.
Someone to stay with me.
Because otherwise, I would have been turned away.
Left in pain because I am alone.

Except I am not.
Not really.

When I opened the front door, Yoshi was there.
Tail wagging gently.
Eyes soft and knowing.
Not asking for anything, only offering presence.

And that is the thing about her.
She never throws stones.
She does not ask, *Why did you not do better?*
She does not say, *You should have taken more time off.*
She does not sigh or huff or roll her eyes.
She simply says, without words, *I am here. I have got you.*

The nurse at the walk-in clinic recently did not have that grace.
She saw the dressing had come loose and launched into blame mode.
Hands on hips. Voice sharp.

'LISTEN,' she snapped. My trigger word.
And just like that, I was a child again. Frozen.
Willing myself not to cry in front of someone who had already decided I was a nuisance.

I tried to explain.
Tried to say, *I am trying. I am alone. I work. I have no choice.*
But she did not care.

Yoshi and Me

She wrapped my hand in bandages that were not even waterproof and sent me off with a warning:
No more help next time.

Because apparently being alone is a crime.
Needing help is weakness.
And trying, despite everything, is not good enough.

But Yoshi did not care that I was messy and shaking when I got home. She did not judge my sweat-soaked clothes or the bandages I had paid for with the last of my food money.

She did not ask what I had said wrong or why I let it happen again.

She sniffed my hand softly.
Pressed her body against my leg.
Looked up at me as if to say,
'You're safe now.'

People will always be difficult.
Life will always be hard.
There will always be bills, doctors, landlords, pain.

But Yoshi?
Yoshi is joy.
Yoshi is safety.
Yoshi is the quiet voice that says, 'You do not have to be strong for me.'

She never asks for more than I can give.
She does not care if dinner is late.
She does not need explanations when I cry.
She only wants to be near me: to walk beside me, nap beside me, exist beside me.

Her only demands are simple:
Treats.
Cuddles.
Play.
Love.
That is all.

And in return, she gives me everything.
She is my teammate.
Not the kind who cheers when I am on top of the world,
but the kind who digs through the dirt to find me when I have fallen.

She is the reason I get up.
The reason I try again tomorrow.
The reason I have not given up, even when every other part of life tells me I should.

The world may always throw rocks.
But she never will.
She just brings them back like treasures.
Drops them at my feet with that silly grin, as if to say,
'Look what I found. Is it not cool?'

And somehow, in her world, even the worst days are softened.
Even the sharp edges begin to smooth out.
Because with her, I am not alone.
With her, I am enough.
With her, I am whole.

Yoshi and Me

 **Pawnote**

Managing Training While Managing Pain

Training when you are chronically ill:

- Use 'training moments' during your day:

    lead on = practise sit,

    mealtime = reinforce calm,

    bathroom = crate time

- Keep sessions short, even 30 seconds. Repeat later.

Energy-saving structure:

- Morning: slow sniff walks and food puzzle.
- Midday: rest (for both of you).
- Evening: tug, trick, or a short play session.

Teething tricks:

- Frozen carrots, wet washcloths from the freezer, or rubber chews filled with broth. Always supervise to ensure your puppy is only chewing items that are safe and not edible. These help to numb the irritation of teething.
- Rotate toys and chews regularly to keep novelty high.

Limit the guilt:

You will not get everything perfect, and that is okay. Focus on relationship, not results.

Yoshi and Me

CHAPTER 17

Breeder vs Rescue: I Just Wanted the Right Dog

This was not about a pet. It was about survival.

🐾 What I Was Really Looking For

When I started planning for an assistance dog, I did not take it lightly. This was not just about getting a companion. It was about finding a partner, someone who could help me manage anxiety, medical episodes, public spaces, and the chaos that disability brings into everyday life.

So I set out to find the right dog.

🐶 Trying the Rescue Route

I started with rescue organisations.

I contacted multiple groups and explained what I needed:

- A young dog
- Calm temperament
- Trainable
- Emotionally stable
- Preferably under two years old

They were kind, supportive, and honest. But they were also realistic.

Most said they had nothing suitable. The only dog anyone suggested was a nine-year-old.

And as much as I wanted to say yes, my heart could not ignore the facts. Training an assistance dog takes time, often years. Starting with a senior dog meant starting over again far too soon.

It would not have been fair. Not to me. Not to them.

🐾 Looking for a Breeder

So I turned to breeders. And I did not go in blind. I researched. Called trainers. Asked about breeds suited for assistance work. I looked up coat types, health risks, and temperament traits.

Everything pointed to one possibility: a Toy Groodle.

They were described as:

- Small.
- Intelligent.
- Allergy-friendly.
- Easy to train.
- Great for public access work.

So I searched. And I found a breeder listed on a 'reputable' dog website, one that claimed to verify all sellers. It gave me confidence.

I asked all the hard questions:

- Health checks?
- Socialisation?
- Parent temperament?
- Early environment?
- Assistance dog potential?

They said everything right.
Yes, they would pick a pup for assistance work.
Yes, they were reputable, responsible, and registered.

So I paid the deposit.
I thought I was doing everything right.

💔 What Actually Happened

What I got was not the right breed.
The support disappeared.
The breeder was gone.
The platform that claimed to be safe? It did nothing.

It still stings.
But even with all that, I do not regret trying.

Because here is the truth no one wants to say out loud: Getting a rescue dog is not always the right option for every disabled person. And choosing a breeder does not guarantee a perfect outcome.

💖 Why I Still Stand by My Choice

I did not choose a breeder out of ego or laziness.
I chose one after every rescue organisation said they could not help.
Because I needed to give myself the best chance I could.

It did not go the way I planned.
But I still got Yoshi.

And maybe, just maybe, that was the plan all along.

🐾 Pawnote

Rescue vs Breeder — There Is No One Path

Rescue Pros:
- You may find a brilliant dog with potential.
- You are giving a second chance.
- Lower upfront cost.

Rescue Cons:
- Unknown history or trauma.
- Fewer suitable puppies.
- Health issues may not appear early.

Breeder Pros:
- Predictability in size, coat, and temperament.
- Chance to meet the litter and see the environment.
- Health and temperament testing available.

Breeder Cons:
- Very expensive.
- No guarantees.
- Scams exist, even on 'reputable' sites.

Red Flags:
- Refusal to let you visit.
- No questions asked of you.

- Avoids paperwork.
- Pressure to 'hurry' or lose the pup.

Green Lights:

- Puppies raised indoors with people.
- Engaged, clean mother.
- Full transparency.
- Offers support after sale.

Reality Check:

Even when you do everything 'right', things can still go wrong. That is not your fault.

A Thought:

Sometimes the 'wrong dog' turns out to be the exact dog you needed. Just like Yoshi.

CHAPTER 18

Owner-Trained vs Organisation-Trained: Choosing Our Own Path

We did not choose this route to be brave. We chose it because it was the only one left.

What I Thought Would Happen

At the beginning, I thought I had options.
Would I get a fully trained dog from an organisation?
Or owner-train one myself?

But it was not really a choice.
Because for me, the organisations never opened the door.

Organisation-Trained Dogs (If You Can Get One)

What is Great:

- Trained by professionals
- Dogs carefully selected for temperament and health

- Often includes paperwork for public access
- Less daily training responsibility for the handler

What is Not:

- Waitlists of two to five years
- Not always available for psychiatric or sensory disabilities
- Breed, type, and training are not tailored to you
- 'Free' is not really free (hidden travel, equipment, and follow-up costs)

And for me? It was not a real option.
Some organisations said no.
Some never replied.
Some did not accept psychiatric needs.
The door was not even cracked open.

🐾 The Owner-Trained Route: Scary, but Ours

When the only option left is to train your own assistance dog, you do not take it lightly. But you take it. Because survival does not wait for waitlists.

What is Good:

- Bonding starts early
- Custom training for your exact needs
- You set the pace
- Sometimes more affordable (but not always)

What is Hard:

- You do everything
- Emotional toll is huge
- Takes one and a half to three years
- No built-in public access recognition, so you must advocate constantly

Owner-Trained vs Organisation-Trained: Choosing Our Own Path

And the truth?
Most of us who owner-train do not do it because we are brave.
We do it because no one else will help.

There Are Some Support

Programmes such as PATDOGS Australia exist to support people who are owner-training.

They will not train the dog for you, but they can:

- Offer public access assessments.
- Provide legitimacy through guidance and structure.
- Help you connect with a community.

The costs are mostly out of pocket or funded if you have access to suitable funding and if that funding allows for their services. They are happy to chat and help arrange access if possible.

Most days, it is still just me and Yoshi, figuring it out in real time while living in survival mode.

🐕 Real, Not Perfect

Yoshi is not perfect.
Neither am I.
But she is real.
She is working.
She is learning.
She is mine.

And even though we did not choose this path, we walk it the best we can.
One paw.
One day.
One task at a time.

CHAPTER 19

What They Don't Tell You About Owner-Training

Everyone sees the dog. No one sees the sleepless nights, breakdowns, or reheated chicken in your pocket.

They will tell you it is rewarding.
They will say how amazing the bond becomes.
They will cheer you on with You are doing so well.

And they are not wrong.
But they are not telling you everything.

No one tells you that you will cry over lead clips.
That you will wonder if every meltdown, yours or the dog's, is a sign you have failed.
That there will be days you question everything.
That you will start explaining to strangers why your dog is allowed into a café more often than you explain your own existence.

Here is what they do not say.

🐾 You Become the Trainer, Therapist, Dietician, Chauffeur… and Sometimes the Villain.

When you owner-train, you are everything.

The trainer. The handler. The comfort. The boss.
The problem-solver when your dog freezes in the middle of a crossing.
The detective when a behaviour starts slipping.
The motivator when you do not even want to get out of bed yourself.

You will have to make decisions you hate.
Like ending a training session early because you cannot regulate.
Or pushing through because the dog needs to learn something crucial, even when you are burning out.

And sometimes you will feel like the villain for enforcing structure.
Even when it is the most loving thing you can do.

🐾 Everything Smells Like Dog Treats.

Your hands.
Your jacket pockets.
That one pair of jeans you swore you would not ruin, now permanently infused with dried jerky treats and regret.

Training treats are your currency, your cologne, your laundry nightmare.
And yet, they work.
So you adapt. You live with smelly fingers.

🐾 It Is Constant, Even When You Are Tired

There is no off switch.
Every walk is a training walk.

Every toilet break is a chance to reinforce a behaviour.
Every public space is a potential battlefield between being ignored or being challenged.

You are always on.
Even when you are exhausted.
Especially when you are exhausted.

Because your dog is watching. Learning.
From every choice you make.

🐾 Your Progress Is Not Linear (And Neither Is Theirs)

You will hit plateaus.
You will backslide.

Sometimes your dog will nail a task for weeks, then suddenly forget it as if they have never heard the cue in their life.
Sometimes you will be the one who forgets.

That is normal.
But when you are owner-training, you do not always have someone to remind you of that.

So I will say it now:
Regression is not failure.
It is part of learning.
For both of you.

🐾 People Will Stare, Judge, Whisper, or Test You

There will be moments you feel like you are performing in a one-person circus. Walking into a shop becomes a silent challenge: Who will say something? Who will stare? Will I be kicked out?

And even when your dog is perfect, people will still question you:

- Are you training her for someone?
- Where is her vest?
- What is she actually trained to do?
- You do not look disabled…

The pressure to prove your dog's worth, and your own, never stops.

But here is the secret:
You do not have to prove anything.
You are already doing more than most could imagine.

🐾 The Magic Happens Quietly

In between the breakdowns and the bone-deep tiredness, something shifts.

Your dog starts doing the thing.
The thing you trained for weeks, months, maybe a year.

They do it in public, unprompted, and suddenly it is not just training anymore.
It is working.
It is real.

You lock eyes, and for a second, all the doubt fades.
You remember why you started.
You remember who you are doing it for.

Not for applause.
Not for proof.
For you.
For them.
For the life you are both building, one cue at a time.

🐾 You Are Not Alone

It can feel isolating, as if everyone else has a team, a budget, a roadmap. But you are not alone.

Every owner-trainer has had a day where they wanted to quit. And every one of us has kept going anyway.

We are the quietly determined. The exhausted but hopeful. The dog-hair-covered warriors teaching our best friends how to change our lives.

One sit-stay.
One task.
One tail wag at a time.

> **Pawnote**
>
> **You Are Doing Hard Things (With a Dog Who Thinks You Are Magic)**
>
> **When it feels like you are falling behind:**
>
> You are not. You are learning. So is your dog.
>
> **When it feels like a rollercoaster:**
>
> That is training. That is disability. That is life.
>
> **When people question you:**
>
> Smile (or do not). You do not owe them an explanation.
>
> **When your dog does the thing:**
>
> Celebrate as if they just won gold at the Assistance Dog Olympics. Because for you, they did.

REMINDER:
You do not need a certificate to be legitimate.
You do not need to be perfect to be enough.
And your dog already thinks you hung the moon.

You are not failing. You are forging a partnership.
And some days, showing up is the bravest, most powerful training you will ever do.

CHAPTER 20

Plateau Brain, Puppy Heart: When Training Feels Stuck

There is a moment in every training journey where things stop working. Not permanently. Just long enough to make you spiral.

We hit that moment a few months into what felt like real progress. Yoshi was smashing cues: *middle*, *under*, *boop*, *chin*, even crowd-control tasks. Then one day… nothing. As if someone had unplugged her brain and swapped it for a gremlin.

And it did not happen just once. It comes in waves.

She will work beautifully one day, then the next she is chasing leaves, ignoring cues, pretending she has never heard the word *sit* in her life. It feels like flipping back to puppy mode. Hello, adolescence again.

It is infuriating. And exhausting. Because when you live with a disability, you are not just training for fun. You are training because you need her to help you function. To go out. To get through a medical episode. To survive the world.

So when she forgets? It feels personal. As if the whole foundation is crumbling.

But then she looks at me. Really looks. And I remember: she has not forgotten me.

She still notices when I start to shut down. She still positions herself between me and the world when I am frozen. She still offers her paw, or rests her head on my knee, or leans against me just enough to say, '*I have got you, even if I am having a strange day*'.

Even in her most chaotic puppy moments, she gives me her bare minimum. And on some days, that is everything. That is enough.

Because I have had people give me nothing. Ignore me. Dismiss me. Hurt me. But Yoshi never walks away.

Even when her training feels like a mess, she always finds a way to stay close. She has never once said *too hard* and disappeared. She has never withheld love. She has never needed me to be anything more than present.

Her memory might be inconsistent. But her loyalty is not.

She shows up, imperfectly but honestly. And so do I.

That is what teamwork really is.

 **Pawnote**

Regression Does Not Mean Rejection

Adolescence in dogs is like a rollercoaster with a gremlin at the wheel. One minute you have a perfect task-doer, the next she is eating grass and ignoring her name.

Regression is part of the process. It is not the end of the road.

Your dog is not testing you. They are growing. And growth is hard, for both of you.

Even on rough days, take note of what your dog still offers:

- One good recall? Win.
- One calm moment? Win.
- The way they check on you when you are not okay? Massive win.

REMEMBER:
You do not have to be perfect.
Your dog does not have to be perfect.
You simply have to keep showing up.

Together.

CHAPTER 21

So You Want to Train Your Own Assistance Dog: Getting Started the Smart Way

So, you have read the stories. You have seen the tasks. You have felt that spark, the one that whispers, Maybe I could do this too.

Welcome. You are officially entering the wonderful, frustrating, joyful, challenging, and deeply personal world of owner-training an assistance dog.

It is not an easy road. But it is a powerful one.

Whether you already have a dog or you are still researching your options, this chapter is your map for the first steps. Not the whole journey, just the starting line. Because no two paths are the same. And that is okay.

First: Is Your Dog a Good Candidate?

Before we look at training tips, let us be honest.
Not every dog is cut out for assistance work.
And that is not a failure, it is a kindness to both you and the dog.

So You Want to Train Your Own Assistance Dog: Getting Started the Smart Way

Here is what to look for in a potential assistance dog:

Age: Ideally under two years old if starting from scratch
Temperament: Calm, confident, human-focused, and recovers quickly from stress
Trainability: Eager to learn, motivated by food or toys, engaged with handler
Health: Vet-checked, sound joints, no major hereditary concerns
Sociability: Enjoys being near people but is not over-excitable

Already have a dog? That is okay too. Just know:

- It is perfectly valid to assess your current dog honestly
- If they are not suited for full public access work, they may still thrive as a home-helper dog
- Some people end up training more than one dog, and learning a great deal with the first

Trainer-Guided or Solo Owner-Trained?

Even in the owner-trainer world, you do not have to do it all alone. You can, and should, seek guidance.

Options to consider:

Path	What It Means	Pros	Cons
Solo Owner-Trained	You design and run the entire program	Cheapest, complete freedom	High risk, legally harder to prove compliance
Trainer-Guided Owner-Trained	You hire a professional for sessions, guidance, and assessments	Support, experience, accountability	Costs add up

Path	What It Means	Pros	Cons
Hybrid Support Program	Join an organisations like PAT Dogs Australia or other organisation available where you live	Structured assessments, public access pathway	May have costs, waitlists, or requirements

Even a few sessions with a good trainer can prevent major mistakes early on.

What to Train First: The Foundation Layer

Here are the first building blocks:

Command	Why It Matters
Name	Builds attention and response
Sit / Down / Stand	Foundation for all future obedience
Wait / Stay	Safety and impulse control
Recall ('Come')	Crucial for safety and off-leash prep
Loose Leash Walking	Makes public outings doable
Leave It / Drop It	Prevents accidents, improves impulse control
Focus / Look at Me	Builds handler engagement
Place / Settle	Teaches calm and rest on cue

Once those are consistent, begin task training based on your needs:

- Interruption of anxiety episodes
- Deep pressure therapy ('over' or 'chin')
- Retrieval or medical alerts

Start **one task at a time**, keep sessions short and positive, and log your progress.

Building Your Training Toolkit

You don't need fancy gear — but the right setup helps.

Training Essentials:

- High-value treats (soft, smelly, varied).
- 1.2m leash + long line (10m for recall practice).
- Front-clip harness for control.
- Mat or towel for 'place'.
- Treat pouch or belt.
- Poop bags.
- Training log (daily notes help you troubleshoot!).

Optional but helpful:

- Clicker or verbal marker like 'Yes!'
- Target stick (for tasks like 'boop' or 'touch').

Where Can You Train?

Start small and build confidence.
Here's a progression example:

1. Home (living room, kitchen)
2. Backyard / driveway
3. Quiet streets / parks
4. Busy Park / carpark (on-leash only)
5. Pet-friendly stores (Bunnings, pet shops)
6. Low-pressure public spaces (libraries, cafés)
7. Complex settings (shopping centres, public transport)

🐾 Generalise each command in at least three to five different environments before moving to new ones.

Legal Stuff to Know in Australia

You don't need to be part of an organisation for your dog to be recognised under the **Disability Discrimination Act 1992 (DDA)** — but your dog must be:

- Trained to perform tasks related to your disability.
- Under control at all times.
- Trained to behave appropriately in public spaces.

That means:
No lunging, barking, jumping.
Toilets only in the right places.
Responds to handler's cues.
Tasks performed on cue, not just vibes.

To avoid access issues:

- Carry a training vest or ID.
- Keep vet/vaccination records.
- Be ready to explain your dog's role without oversharing your diagnosis.

People to Know / Places to Contact

Resource	How They Can Help
Assistance Dog Trainers	Support sessions, task guidance.
PAT Dogs Australia / Mind Dogs	Public Access support, advocacy.

Resource	How They Can Help
Local Councils	Dog registration and by-laws.
NDIS Support Coordinators	If applicable, they may help fund some training.
Facebook Owner-Trainer Groups	Lived experience, troubleshooting, and moral support (with caution: not all advice is equal).

If It Doesn't Go to Plan? That's Okay.

Some dogs need more time.
Some aren't suited.
Sometimes you have to pivot — and that's not a failure.

The fact that you're trying, that you're learning, that you're showing up for your own survival, that's what matters.

> **Pawnote**
>
> **You're Not Behind, You're Just Early**
> - This isn't a race. No-one gets to tell you how fast or slow to go.
> - Trust is built over time. So is teamwork.
> - Some days it will feel like nothing is working. Keep going anyway.
> - You're not a bad trainer. You're just in the messy middle.
> - And you're not alone — not with four paws beside you.

> **Sample Training Log — Assistance Dog in Training**
>
> Keeping a training log is essential. It helps you:
>
> - Track progress.
> - Notice patterns.
> - Identify what's working (or not).
> - Provide evidence if applying for NDIS support or access recognition.

Daily Training Log Template

Date	Time	Focus Area	Cues Practised	Notes / Observations	Outcome
06/08	10–20 mins	(e.g. Public Access, Task Training, Distraction Proofing)	Sit, Down, Boop	Dog distracted by kids, recovered with "focus" cue. Passed trolley calmly.	Progressing / Needs Work / Building

Tips:

- Keep sessions short (5 to 15 mins max).
- End on a success.
- Write down even small wins (they matter).
- Don't train every day — rest is training too.

🛒 Public Access Readiness Checklist

Before taking your dog into public spaces, ensure they can reliably:

Behavioural Checklist

- Sit, Down, and Stay with moderate distractions.
- Loose leash walking in new environments.
- Ignore food on ground or tables.
- Respond to name and handler under stress.
- Settle quietly for 5–10 mins at handler's feet.
- Tolerate loud noises, trolleys, sliding doors.
- Toilet on command and outside.
- No barking, lunging, growling, jumping.
- No begging or sniffing merchandise.
- Remain focused despite people/dogs nearby.
- Allow polite interaction (only if invited).

Task Checklist

- Performs at least one trained task that directly assists with disability.
- Can perform task reliably in at least three locations.
- Recovers from errors without escalating.
- Responds to 'break' or release cue when off duty.

Handler Checklist

- Calm, confident handling.
- Equipment in good condition.
- Carries ID and dog records (vaccination, training log).
- Prepares calming tools (treats, mat, chews).
- Can redirect, remove, or manage dog if overwhelmed.
- Plans short trips with specific goals.

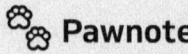 **Pawnote**

Readiness Isn't Perfection

You *don't* need your dog to be a robot.
You *do* need:

- Reliability in essential cues
- Good recovery from distractions
- A strong bond and communication
- A plan for when things don't go to plan

Mistakes will happen.
What matters is how your team handles them — together.

CHAPTER 22

Practising for the Public: The First Outing Is Never the First

The first time you see an assistance dog in public, calmly lying under a café table or weaving through crowds like a professional, it looks effortless — like they were born to do it.

Spoiler: they weren't.

What you're seeing is the result of *hundreds* of small steps, careful planning, failed attempts, and a whole lot of snacks.

Because here's the golden rule of public access work:

The first time your dog goes into a real public space… should never be their actual first time.

We train for it.
We prepare for it.
We rehearse every little part before we do the full thing.

We Make 'Firsts' Happen Before They Count

Before our 'first public outing' to a café, Yoshi had already:

- Walked past cafés with outdoor seating.
- Heard cutlery clatter and chairs scrape.
- Smelled grilled chicken, fries, and a hundred dropped crumbs.
- Practised 'under' on a towel beside me at home and at the park.
- Watched me eat snacks on a park bench without asking for a single bite.
- Settled calmly beside me while I scrolled my phone in the car park.

By the time we walked into that café… she'd already been there a dozen times in her mind.

That's the trick you don't train for public access *in* public.
You train all the parts separately. Then you start stitching them together like a puzzle.

The World Is Loud. We Build Up Slowly

Public places are chaos for a dog.
Trolleys squeak. Kids scream. Alarms go off. People point.
There are smells on smells on smells.

So we expose them to it bit by bit. Like this:

1. Scout the Location Without the Dog
Scope it out first. Where are the entrances, exits, and quiet corners? What are the distractions? Is there shade or seating nearby?

2. Start in Parking Lots or Edges of Busy Areas
You don't walk straight into a mall. You start in the car park. You reward calm for watching trolleys from afar.

3. Practise the Behaviours at Home or Quiet Places First
'Under', 'wait', 'leave it', 'focus', 'middle'.
We teach these in the living room. The backyard. The park. Not inside supermarket for the first time.

4. Do Short Visits with a Clear Goal
It's not 'Let's do the weekly shop.'
It's 'Let's enter, go to the first aisle, turn around, and leave'.
Success = calm entry + calm exit.

Not Every Dog Is Ready Today — and That's Okay

Yoshi has days where she slips back into adolescent mode. She gets distracted. She sniffs a pole too long. She forgets where her butt is when sitting in a narrow aisle.

But she also cares. Even in her chaos, she'll give me the best she can. Some days, that's a calm settle. Other days, it's just staying close and trying not to bounce.

And on those days, that is enough.

We don't rush it. Because an overwhelmed dog is a stressed dog. And a stressed dog doesn't learn — they just survive.

I don't want Yoshi to survive public access.

I want her to feel confident in it.

Public Access Isn't the Goal — It's the Byproduct

Our goal isn't just being allowed into places.
It's having a dog that feels safe, focused, and empowered to help.

That only comes when we train before the big moments.

So no, our 'first' outing wasn't actually our first.

It was our 15th dry run, eighth snack break, third park bench test, and first time she nailed it all at once.

And that's how it should be.

 Pawnote

Firsts Are Built — Not Faced Alone

Don't rush the first:

- First restaurant? Practise at home and parks first.
- First bus? Let them watch one go past. Then sit near the stop. Then ride one for one stop only.
- First shopping centre? Start in the car park. Then the food court entrance. Then short, low-traffic visits.

Make a habit of:

- Pre-walk sniff breaks.
- Parking lot practice.
- Public settle drills (on towel/mat).
- Practising 'under' and 'middle' while seated.

 REMEMBER:
- If your dog is struggling, you are allowed to leave.
- Every 'first' is just the next step in a much longer journey.
- Public access is a privilege earnt through kindness, patience, and preparation for both of you.

Public Access Prep: First Outing Checklist

Because the first public outing should never be the first real one.

Step	Description
Scout the Location (without dog)	Visit the venue alone. Check for: accessible entry, shade, quiet corners, seating, exits, toilet access.
Pre-Exposure Training	Practise key cues at home or in the yard: 'under', 'stay', 'leave it', 'middle', 'focus', 'settle'.
Distraction Conditioning	Visit parking lots, outdoor cafés, and shopfronts. Reward calm watching of people, trolleys, cars, noises.
Mat Training	Practise 'settle' on a towel or mat — in different places like the park, driveway, friend's house, etc.
Noise and Movement	Safely expose your dog to clanging trolleys, scooters, automatic doors, music, children, and carts *before* entering a busy space.
Handler Plan	Know your goal for the visit (e.g., enter → reach aisle 3 → exit). Keep it short and achievable.
Dog Ready?	Has your dog toileted, been exercised, and had calm time beforehand? Bring high-value treats + water.
Quiet Entry Point	Choose a low-traffic time and a side entrance, if possible. Avoid peak hours or busy events for early visits.
Reward Calm on Entry	Reinforce check-ins, loose leash walking, calm breathing. Be ready to redirect or exit if overstimulated.
Quick Exit Plan	Know when to call it. If it's not going well, leave before it escalates. Praise your dog anyway.

TIPS FOR SUCCESS:

- **Start small.** A quiet pharmacy or bookstore < massive shopping centre.
- **Keep visits short.** First real outings should be under 10 to 15 minutes.
- **Track progress.** Log each visit and rate focus, stress, and responsiveness.
- **Use familiar items.** Bring the same towel/mat they've practised on at home.

CHAPTER 23

Not Quite Ready: But Getting Closer

There is this quiet, unspoken pressure when you are training an assistance dog. As if people expect perfection from day one. As if you are only valid if your dog is flawless in a vest, already passing every test with a wagging tail and a medical degree.

But truthfully?
We are not ready. Not fully.

Yoshi has not passed her Public Access Test yet.
And that is okay.

She is still young, only sixteen months, and she has already done more than most dogs her age. She passed her learner-level obedience requirements, the *L-plates*, at around eight months old. That is no small feat. It means she can sit calmly, walk nicely, and respond reliably in all sorts of everyday situations.

But we are not rushing the final hurdle.

She is brilliant in vet clinics. She sits patiently as if she owns the place. She comes to work with me occasionally and behaves the best she can for a full seven hours. She has done training runs at local shops, short visits to cafés, and has even handled crowded car parks and automatic doors like a pro.

And some days she nails it.
Other days we both want to bolt the second a toddler screams or a trolley rattles past.

Because she is still an adolescent.
And honestly, so am I, in healing.

We are training.
We are learning.
We are growing, together.

Yoshi started life unsure of the world.
And here she is, learning to help me survive in a world I also find terrifying.

So no, our first outing will not really be our first.
Because we have been laying the groundwork the whole time.
And when the big day comes, we will both know we are ready.

> 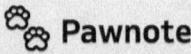 **Pawnote**
>
> **Progress Is Not a Race**
> - Early achievement does not mean early pressure
> - Give your dog time to mature emotionally
> - Confidence is built through consistency, not speed

- It is okay to pause, to go back, to slow down
- You are not behind, you are becoming
- 'In training' still means worthy
- Celebrate the wins: vet visits, loose lead walks, recovery after distractions
- You do not need to prove anything to anyone else
- The goal is not perfection. The goal is partnership.

CHAPTER 24

Why We're Not Rushing the Test

Yes, Yoshi has an ID card.

It says 'Assistance Dog In Training.' Because she is with an organisation and follows their syllabus, we're allowed everywhere except on planes or in sterile areas like operating theatres.

It lives in my pocket like a little shield, ready to be shown when someone stops us with a stare or a question.

But people act like that card is the finish line — as if passing the Public Access Test (which is not even mandatory in most states yet) magically turns your dog into a perfectly polished, push-button miracle machine.

Perfect. Predictable. Done.

But that is not how this works.
That is not how we work.

Yoshi is already doing the job.
She is not waiting for a laminated card to tell her when to help.

Why We're Not Rushing the Test

She reads my body language before I even notice I am spiralling.
She nudges me back when I start to float.
She braces quietly in noisy shops when my knees wobble.
She leans across me like a weighted blanket when my brain short-circuits.
And somehow, she knows exactly when to just be near.

The Public Access Test?
That is paperwork.
A technicality.
A badge for work she already shows up for, every single day.

According to our trainer Tamika, she could pass it soon.
But she is only sixteen months old.
And I want her to grow into this, not simply perform for it.

I want her to flop on her back in the sun.
To dig holes.
To sniff every tree and chase every fluttering leaf as if it were the grand prize.

She has earned that.
We have trained hard.
She has passed her obedience.
Handled vet clinics like a pro.
Completed short, successful public outings.
And she has done it all with heart, courage, and tail-wagging joy.

We are not skipping steps.
We are simply walking them at our pace.
Letting her be a dog, while she grows into the dog I need.

So when the day comes, we will not be nervous.
We will be ready.
Not just to pass, but to thrive.

And yet, even with that little ID card, the questions come.

'Is she certified?'
'What is she trained to do?'
'Are you allowed to bring her here?'

Here is the truth.

That card did not teach her how to spot a shutdown before it happens.
It did not help her recover from fear reactivity.
It did not teach her how to anchor me in a crowd.
It did not teach her to sit through hours of medical appointments, therapy lobbies, or pharmacy queues.

We did that.
Together.

The card might prove something on paper.
But it is the bond between us that does the real work.
The quiet trust. The everyday effort. The countless hours of showing up, even when neither of us feels ready.

And no, we have not passed the Public Access Test yet.
But that does not stop Yoshi from doing her job.

Because assistance dogs do not wait for a certificate to start saving your life.
They just show up.
Every single day.
Unconditionally.

Why We're Not Rushing the Test

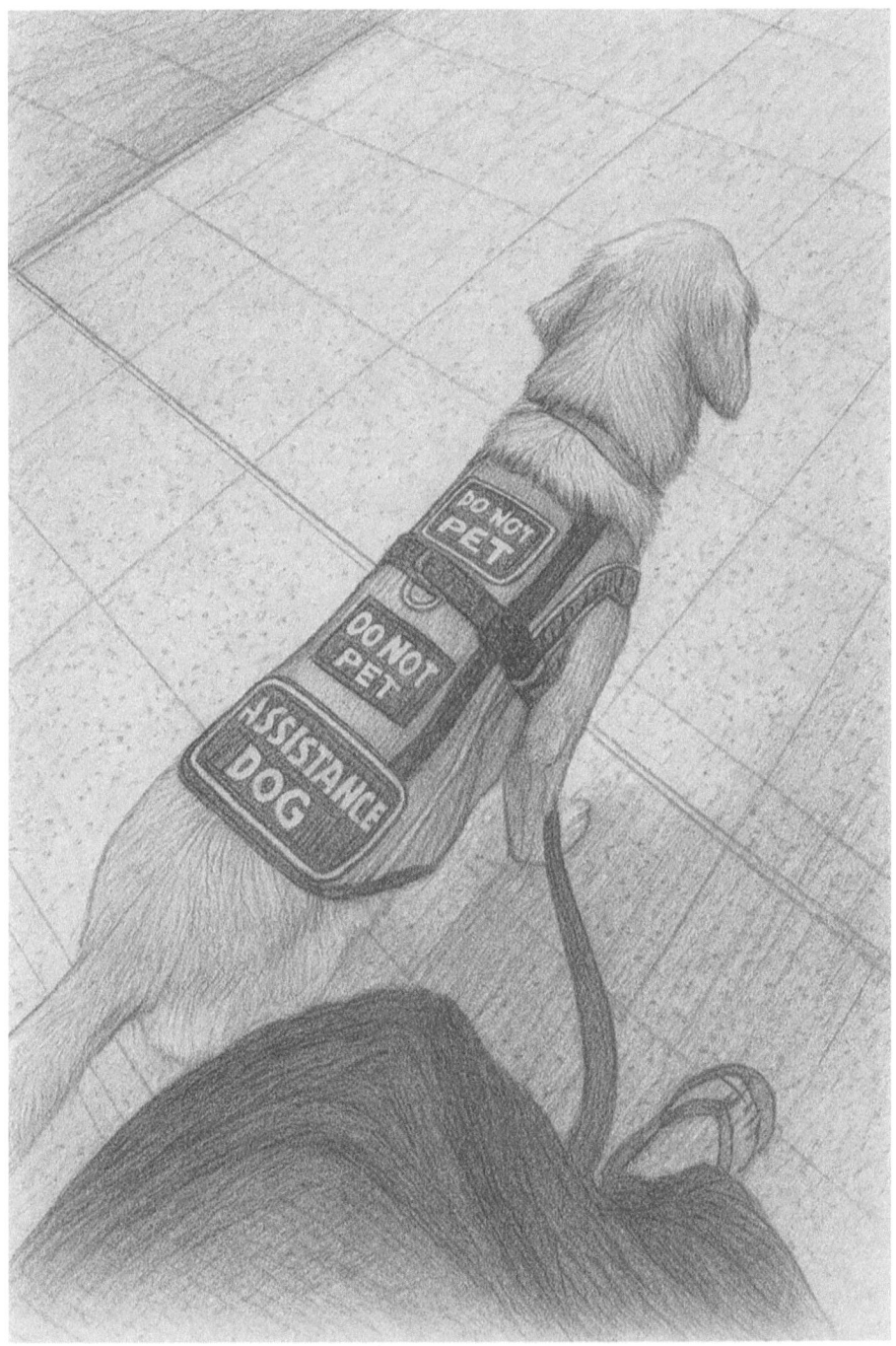

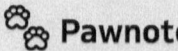 **Pawnote**

The Vest Does Not Prove the Bond

- ID cards may help with access, but they do not define the partnership
- Public access is not a one-time test, it is a daily practice in a messy world
- Do not let someone's curiosity or ignorance shake your confidence
- The real work happens long before the paperwork, long before the vest
- What matters most: trust, consistency, and showing up together

CHAPTER 25

Training Through the Spiral

There is this little gremlin in your head that pops up the moment something goes wrong.
You drop a lead. Miss a cue. Your dog barks. You panic.

And suddenly that gremlin whispers, You are not good enough. You have ruined everything.

Let us be very clear about something:
Mistakes are part of the process.
Yours. Your dog's. Everyone's.

Assistance dogs are not born knowing how to navigate shopping centres and public transport. And you were not born knowing how to train one.

Even the most experienced handlers have bad days. Dogs regress. Handlers burn out. Life throws a dozen things at you all at once and suddenly everything you have worked for feels like it is slipping.

Yoshi has had days where her brain simply vanishes.
She forgets how to sit. She forgets she is not supposed to lunge toward

another dog to say hello.
And I forget how to breathe.

But we always come back.
We sit. We cuddle. We try again.

Why Mistakes Happen

- **Adolescence:** that stage between puppy and adult where brains are mush and impulse control is optional
- **Environment:** loud noises, smells, unpredictable people it is a lot to deal with
- **Health:** your dog might be tired, sore, or overstimulated; so might you
- **Training gaps:** sometimes you think you have taught a behaviour, but not in that situation

When Things Go Wrong

- Pause, breathe, check in with your dog
- Ask: are they struggling or confused? Am I okay?
- Use the moment as data, not a verdict
- Leave early if needed; there is no shame in retreating with dignity

What Helps

- Keep a training journal, write down the good and the bad
- Build decompression time into your schedule
- Talk to your trainer or support group; not every wobble means failure
- Have a recovery ritual: ice cream, films from the sofa, sniffy walks — whatever works
- Forgive yourself. Often

Because here is the truth:
Your dog will mess up.
You will mess up.
But what matters is not the mistake, it is what you do next.

Yoshi has never held my bad day against me.
She simply checks in, rests her chin on my lap, and says with her eyes, 'We are still a team, yes?'

Yes. We are.

 Pawnote

Regressions Are Not Failures

- A barking dog is not a broken dog, it is communication
- A shutdown handler is not incompetent, they are overwhelmed
- Progress is a squiggly line, not a staircase
- Breathe. You are allowed to learn as you go

CHAPTER 26

Where to Next: Building Toward Certification (If That's Your Goal)

So, you have been training. Your dog is getting pretty solid. You have survived the teething, the meltdowns, the awkward vet waiting room moments. Maybe they are already helping you with daily tasks. Maybe they have saved your sanity more times than you can count.

And now you are wondering:
What comes next?
Do I need certification?
How do I prove my dog is legitimate?

Let us be real for a moment.
Certification is not a legal requirement in Australia.

Under the **Disability Discrimination Act 1992**, if your dog is trained to assist you with your disability and behaves appropriately in public, you already have rights. But in reality, the public, businesses, and even some government departments often do not understand that.

That is where the **Public Access Test (PAT)** comes in.

What Is the PAT?

The Public Access Test is a standardised way to assess whether your assistance dog can behave reliably in public. It checks:

- Obedience and responsiveness
- Calm behaviour in busy or noisy environments
- Safe toileting practices
- Handler control and teamwork

Passing a PAT gives your dog recognition as *public access ready* — a massive help when navigating the world of stares, questions, and denied entries.

But here is the challenge. Even if you pass, it is not forever.

In Australia, you must re-sit the PAT every twelve months to maintain certification. That means staying sharp, continuing training, and proving again and again that your dog is capable and appropriate for public work.

Is Certification Right for You?

Here is the truth. Certification does not make your dog more of an assistance dog. It simply makes it easier to prove it to others.

If your dog is already trained and doing the job, that is excellent. But if you want smoother access, formal assessments, or the support of an organisation for backup, here are your options.

Australia-Wide Assistance Dog Organisations That Support Owner-Trainers

These groups either assess or support the journey of owner-trainers. Many offer Public Access Tests, ID cards, community, and guidance. Some also assist with re-certification.

Organisation	Description
PATDOGS Australia	National PAT provider for owner-trainers. Offers assessments, ID cards, and trainer-led reviews.
MindDog Australia	Focuses on psychiatric assistance dogs. Requires significant training documentation, assessments, and team suitability.
GHAD (Guide Hearing & Assistance Dogs QLD)	Queensland-based but open to some owner-trainers for testing and recognition.
Smart Pups (QLD)	Offers support and assessments primarily for families with children on the autism spectrum.
Assistance Dogs International (ADI)	Accredits organisations, not individuals—but if your dog is trained by one, they're automatically recognised.

 PLEASE NOTE: We are not recommending any specific organisation or suggesting which to choose. Please do your own research. This list is accurate as of August 2025.

🦴 Note: Every organisation has different rules. Some require you to use their trainers. Others need a logbook, video evidence, or letters from allied health professionals. Some charge an annual membership. Always check before applying.

So… Am I Ready?

Here's a rough guide to help you check in with yourself:

🐾 Public Access Readiness Checklist

- My dog can stay calm in public.
- My dog ignores food, other dogs, and people when working.
- My dog is toilet-trained for long outings.
- I can give clear, consistent commands.
- I can advocate for myself and my dog if questioned.
- We can both recover after a stressful public moment.
- We have practised in a variety of locations (shops, public transport, footpaths, etc.).
- My dog performs trained tasks that directly assist with my disability.
- I have spoken to a trainer or assessor for feedback.
- I understand that this is a 12-month certification and not a one-and-done test.

But What If I'm Not Ready Yet?

That is okay. Truly.
You do not need to rush. This is not a race.

Some dogs pass at twelve months.
Some at three years.
Some never sit a PAT at all and still work beautifully as assistance animals.

Focus on building the bond.
Work on real-life situations.
Get help from trainers who understand assistance dog work.
And when you are ready, you will know.

 **Pawnote**

Certification Is a Stepping Stone, Not a Summit

- You do not need a certificate to be a team.
- But it can help with public life and peace of mind.
- Support exists; you do not have to do this alone.
- Retesting every twelve months is not a burden, it is a check-in.
- The goal is not a piece of paper. The goal is partnership.

Am I Ready?
A Simple Flowchart

Thinking of Getting a Dog?
↓
Am I ready for a dog?
(Stable housing, time, money, support)
↓
Do I need this dog for assistance work?
↓
What breed and where to get the dog from responsibly?
↓
Do I know what tasks I need help with?
↓
Can I train the dog myself or get help from trainers?
↓
Do I already have a dog?
↓
Is the dog suitable for public access work?
(Calm, confident, friendly temperament)
↓
Has training already started?
↓
Is my dog ready for the Public Access Test (PAT)?
↓
Can my dog:
- Stay calm in public?
- Ignore distractions?
  - Toilet on cue?
- Perform trained tasks?
- Recover from stress?

↓

→ **YES** → You're ready to consider a PAT! Reach out to an assessor or organisation.

→ **NO** → Keep training and bonding. You're doing great!

CHAPTER 27

Intro to Advanced Training, Tasks and Troubleshooting

Training does not stop at *sit*. It just becomes more creative.

We have come a long way from luring her into a sit with a scrap of chicken and calling it a win. Now we are deep in the world of advanced tasks, where timing matters, emotions seep into everything, and distractions come in loud, spicy, or sausage-roll form.

Chaining Behaviours

Want your dog to perform complex tasks such as go get a bottle of water, bring it to me, and nudge me to drink? That is called task chaining: teaching each piece of a multi-step behaviour, then linking them together.

Yoshi has done early versions of this, such as:

- Go to the door
- Pick up the lead
- Bring it to me
- Sit and wait for cue

We do not always get all the pieces in one go. Sometimes she grabs a shoe instead of the lead. Sometimes she brings both. Once, she even brought the broom.

We celebrate the tries.
We train the steps.
And we laugh in between.

Generalising Behaviours

Your dog might perform a perfect down-stay at home… and completely forget it exists at the park.
That is normal.

Generalising means teaching your dog that the cue works anywhere, not just in the lounge room. So we practise cues:

- At the shops
- Outside vet clinics
- On damp grass
- Near skateboards
- While someone drops a meat pie

We practise with distractions, not against them.

Adding Duration, Distance, and Distractions (3Ds)

A sit that lasts one second at your feet is very different from:

- Sitting for two minutes
- While you walk away
- While a bike goes past
- On unfamiliar ground

We build slowly, one 'D' at a time. If she breaks the stay, we reset. No punishment, just a reminder: we are learning.

Troubleshooting Common Problems

Barking

Yoshi does not bark much now, but adolescence came with a few surprise outbursts. The triggers?

- A flapping banner
- Balloons
- That one bin near the pharmacy

Instead of scolding her, I asked why she was barking. Was she scared? Uncertain? Over-aroused?
Then we trained for it.
Distance. Rewards. 'Look at that'.
It worked better than 'shhhhh'.

Sniffing

Sometimes we walk.
Sometimes we stop at every single scent.

And honestly, that is fine, unless we are mid-task or somewhere sniffing is unsafe. We trained sniff time versus working time. Sniffing is allowed when released, not during focused cues such as *heel* or *under*. It is not perfect, but we are communicating.

Overexcitement

It still happens, whether she is around certain people, other dogs, or simply tired and overstimulated.

The full tail-spin launch sequence.

And when it happens in a shop or waiting room, we pause and reset.
No shouting. No shame.
We breathe together.
And sometimes we leave and try again tomorrow.

When to Call in Help Again

There is no shame in needing support.

If your dog:

- Suddenly develops new behaviours
- Seems stressed or shut down
- Regresses for weeks, not just a one-off
- Stops responding to cues in multiple settings
- Displays aggression, fear, or compulsive behaviour

…it is time to seek input from a trainer, behaviourist, or vet.

Even without problems, sometimes you just want fresh eyes or a confidence boost.

We still check in with Tamika. Sometimes just to say Look what she did! Sometimes to ask, Okay… what do I do now? And every time, we leave feeling seen and supported.

> **Pawnote**
>
> **You're Not Behind**
>
> - You do not need to 'fix' everything overnight
> - Regression does not mean failure, it means your dog needs help
> - A sniff is not disobedience, it is communication
> - You are allowed to ask for help, even if you have come this far on your own

Advanced Task Samples

Advanced Task 1: Pick It Up and Bring It to Me

(Object retrieval for items such as water bottles, keys, and similar objects)

Step-by-Step Task Chain

Step	Behaviour	How to Train It
1	Target the object	Use a clicker or treat to shape interest in the object (for example, keys). Reward for looking, then sniffing, then touching.
2	Mouth and hold	Encourage gently mouthing or holding the object using a cue such as *Take it*. Begin with soft-textured toys if needed, then gradually switch to the real item.
3	Lift the object	Shape the lifting movement. Reward even the smallest attempts. Progress until your dog can lift and hold it reliably.
4	Move toward you	Stand close. Cue 'bring' or 'come'. Reward when your dog brings the item part of the way. Slowly increase the distance.
5	Place it in your hand or lap	Teach a 'give' or 'drop' cue with your hand as the target. Reinforce gently dropping it into your hand or lap, rather than at your feet.
6	Chain all steps	Put all the cues together into one task. Give the cue, "Yoshi, get the keys." and reward with praise and a treat when she completes it. Add a visual cue if needed.

Intro to Advanced Training, Tasks and Troubleshooting

 TIPS FOR SUCCESS

- Start with soft, safe objects before moving to real ones such as metal keys or bottles
- Use clicker training or a marker word such as *yes!* to mark each success
- Keep sessions short and fun; do not train to frustration
- If your dog drops the item on the way, pause, encourage, and reset

Real Life Example

You drop the lead and cannot bend over.
You say, "Yoshi, get the lead".
She looks down, picks it up, and drops it gently into your hand.
You say *Yes!* and reward her with a piece of chicken.
She wags her tail as if she has just won the dog Olympics.

And in her way, she has.

Advanced Task 2: Interrupting Anxiety or Panic Behaviours
(Nudge Me or Check on Me)

What It Does

The dog notices repetitive stress signs (such as fidgeting, rocking, or zoning out) and nudges you back to awareness.

How to Train:

1. Teach 'Nudge'
    - Hold a treat in your fist.
    - Say nudge and let your dog touch their nose to your hand.
    - Mark ('yes' or click) and reward.
    - Repeat until your dog nudges on cue.
2. Pair with a Behaviour
    - Mimic a real stress behaviour (such as hand-wringing).
    - Cue your dog to nudge while you do it
    - Mark and reward.
    - Gradually fade the verbal cue so the dog responds to the stress action alone.
3. Add Realism
    - Begin training when you are mildly anxious (not distressed).
    - Gradually work up to more intense versions.
    - Keep rewarding calm, consistent responses.
4. Generalise
    - Practise in different locations and positions (sitting, lying down).
    - Reward your dog for spotting the behaviour and responding early.

> **TIP**
> If you are prone to dissociation or freezing, train your dog to nudge repeatedly until you respond. Use a release cue such as 'am okay' so they know when the job is complete.

Advanced Task 3: Blocking in Public Spaces (Block / Cover)

What It Does

The dog stands in front, beside, or behind you to prevent people from getting too close. This creates space, comfort, and a sense of control.

How to Train

1. Teach Position
   - Use a treat to lure your dog to stand in front of you, facing away
   - Say 'block' when they are in position
   - Mark and reward, repeating until fluent
   - Practise the same movement behind you with the cue *cover*
2. Add Duration
   - Ask for 'block' or 'cover'.
   - Wait one to two seconds before rewarding.
   - Slowly build the time your dog holds the position.
3. Add Distance
   - Take one step away.
   - Return and reward if they hold the position.
   - Gradually increase the distance.
4. Add Real-World Practice
   - Begin in a quiet park, then move to a footpath, then near a shop queue.
   - Use high-value rewards, as this requires focus.
5. Add Cue Without Luring
   - Once fluent, give the cue *block* or *cover* without luring.
   - Reward heavily when they perform it independently.

TIP

Keep sessions short and end on a success. This task builds confidence and connection. Always finish training with cuddles or play. You are asking your dog to help during difficult moments, so make it a joyful job.

CHAPTER 28

Becoming, Together

When I first brought Yoshi home, I did not know what we were stepping into.
I did not know if I was doing the right thing.
I did not know if I would be strong enough to train an assistance dog, let alone survive all the hurdles life kept throwing my way.
I did not even know if I would still be here.

But somehow, one paw at a time, we found a way forward.

This book has taken you through the early chaos and cuddles, the trauma and trust-building, the training sessions that ended in tears, and the victories that felt like miracles. We have covered enrichment and adolescence, obedience and outings, legal barriers and emotional breakthroughs.

We have shared what it means to choose each other, every single day.

Yoshi has not just grown into her job. She has grown into herself.
And in many ways, so have I.

We are not perfect.

She still chases leaves sometimes.
I still get overwhelmed in the cereal aisle.
There are meltdowns. There are regressions.

But there is also magic. So much magic.

Because no matter what else is happening in the world, Yoshi still comes back to me.
And I still reach for her.

We are a team.
Not just because of what we do.
But because of who we are to each other.

And while this may be the end of the book, it is not the end of the journey.
There are more adventures ahead.
More training.
More play.
More days where simply surviving is enough.
More people to meet, more spaces to open, more lessons to learn — together.

So if you are starting your own assistance dog journey, or you are somewhere in the messy middle, I hope this gave you comfort. Or clarity. Or just a reminder that you are not alone.

Because at the heart of it all is this simple truth:
We are not training perfect dogs.
We are building imperfect, beautiful partnerships.

And that takes time.
Patience.
Compassion.

And above all, love.

Thank you for being part of ours.

We are still becoming.
And that is more than enough.

📚 Appendix: Legal Information – Australia

Laws and policies may change over time. As of August 2025, this information reflects current regulation—but always check your local government or official site for the most up-to-date details.

📄 Disability Discrimination Act 1992 (Commonwealth)

➤ *Website:* www.legislation.gov.au

This federal law provides foundational protection for people with disabilities—and their assistance dogs. Under Section 9, the presence of a trained, well-behaved assistance animal cannot be used as a basis for discrimination across public spaces, services, housing, education, or employment.

📄 Australian Human Rights Commission – Assistance Animals

➤ *Website:* www.humanrights.gov.au

The AHRC supports DDA compliance and handles disputes when access is denied. They offer:

- Guidelines and legal advice for handlers
- Complaint procedures for inappropriate refusal
- Useful tips for advocating in public settings

⚲ Overview: State and Territory Legal Requirements

Below is a snapshot of policies as of August 2025. Individual councils or venues can still have specific rules and documentation requests.

Region	Requires State Access ID?	Public Register Exists?	Protected by DDA?
NSW	No	No	✓ Yes
VIC	Sometimes	Indirect	✓ Yes
QLD	✓ Yes	✓ Yes	✓ Yes
WA	✓ Yes	✓ Yes	✓ Yes
SA	No	No	✓ Yes
TAS	No	No	✓ Yes
ACT	No	No	✓ Yes
NT	No	No	✓ Yes

🏢 State/Territory Notes in Brief

- New South Wales (NSW): No central registration, but local councils may require proof of training.
- Victoria (VIC): Accreditation must align with DDA; some providers offer certification pathways.
- Queensland (QLD): Has formal state certification and ID system via Guide, Hearing and Assistance Dog Act of 2009 (GHAD).
- Western Australia (WA): Assistance Dog Permit required under Dog Act 1976.
- South Australia (SA), Tasmania (TAS), ACT, NT: No formal state register; DDA protection applies. Always travel with documentation.

Tips for Handlers

- Keep an ID card, training log, vet history, and emergency contact information on your phone or in a small binder.
- Print or screenshot the relevant webpage or PDF for your state's regulations to carry discreetly.
- Know what the Disability Discrimination Act 1992 covers—especially your right to bring your assistance dog into public spaces.
- If you feel access has been unfairly denied, *document the incident* and consider filing a complaint or seeking support through the Australian Human Rights Commission.

 Pawnote

Laws Change — But Responsibilities Stay

- Always verify local rules before moving interstate or accessing new venues.
- A policy change doesn't negate the bonds and training you've built. It just means adapting.
- Regardless of certification or ID types, the law protects you. You still have rights.
- If you encounter resistance, you're not alone—and there are pathways to advocate for yourself.

EPILOGUE

Still Here, Still Us

When I started this journey, I did not know if I would make it through the hard days. I did not know if I would manage the pain, the flare-ups, the breathless nights. I did not know if Yoshi would understand me, or if I would be able to understand her.

Now, we read each other without words.

Recently, when my lungs gave in with an autoimmune flare, virus, and bronchitis all tangled together, she knew before I did. She rested her chin and paw on my upper arm. Five minutes later, the coughing storms would hit. The pulse oximeter confirmed it: oxygen in the eighties, heart rate climbing to one hundred and fifty to one hundred and sixty, the danger zone where you are meant to head for Emergency.

It felt like standing in the middle of wreckage again, but this time I was not alone.

Yoshi did not just warn me. She learnt to help. Two demonstrations, and she could fetch my puffer. Sometimes still hit and miss, but enough to make the difference between panic and breathing again.

And it is not just my lungs. She knows when I am slipping into autistic restlessness such as the fidgeting or the chest-hitting tic. She starts small: chin down, then a paw. If I do not stop, she escalates, jumping up to press both paws into my arms until I pause.

We still make mistakes. She still asks for help sometimes, and I still give her the chance to work it out first. But we keep showing up for each other.

Out on the trails, she runs but always comes back. She asks permission before greeting most dogs now, nine times out of ten, a quiet nod to the trust between us.

I need her. I love her. She is the golden thread running through the chaos of my life, holding the pieces together when everything else tries to fall apart.

We are still learning. Still growing. Still breathing together.

And if we can do that, so can you.

And as the day closes, we walk home side by side, four paws and two tired feet, moving in step, ready for whatever comes next.

🐾 About the Author

Yevette did not set out to become a dog trainer, behaviour enthusiast, or assistance dog handler. Life simply had other plans. After years of navigating the world with invisible disabilities, chronic illness, and trauma, she found herself face to snout with a golden retriever named Yoshi, and everything changed.

Raising and training Yoshi from puppyhood, Yevette took on the immense challenge of building an owner-trained assistance dog from scratch. No big organisation. No fancy resources. Just a deep bond, unwavering persistence, and a great deal of trial and error.

Today, Yoshi is seventeen months old and already performs a wide range of disability-related tasks with heart, intuition, and a tail that never stops wagging.

Yevette is currently completing her Certificate IV in Animal Behaviour and Training with a specialisation in assistance dog work, and she also holds a Certificate IV in Training and Assessment, reflecting her strong background in coaching and education. She is mentored by a highly experienced assistance dog trainer and behaviourist, who continues to support and guide her journey.

Her hands-on experience also includes time spent in a doggy daycare, grooming, and boarding facility, where she worked with everything from pampered poodles to mischief-making mutts, as well as the less glamorous side of the job. These experiences gave her insight into a wide range of breeds, behaviours, and challenges, both canine and human.

Now, Yevette helps others on their own journey, whether they are wondering if their dog has the potential to become an assistance dog, need support with basic training or behavioural challenges, or are only beginning to explore what an assistance dog could mean for their life.

Through everything, she has learned that the most powerful tools are not just cues and commands. They are compassion, patience, and connection.

This book is a raw, honest, and sometimes hilarious reflection of her lived experience. It is not a manual. It is a messy, beautiful blueprint for those walking a similar path, especially those walking it alone.

📷 **Follow Yoshi's journey**
Instagram:@yoshipawsad
Facebook: YoshiPawsAD